DEAR SAM

To Sue –
A bestest friend
if there ever was one.
Love,
Janet
(aka Wife #2)

DEAR SAM

Grieving the Death of My Son

a memoir

JANET TORGE

iUniverse, Inc.
New York Lincoln Shanghai

DEAR SAM
Grieving the Death of My Son

iUniverse books may be ordered through booksellers or by contacting:

iUniverse
2021 Pine Lake Road, Suite 100
Lincoln, NE 68512
www.iuniverse.com
1-800-Authors (1-800-288-4677)

The views expressed in this work are solely those of the author and do not necessarily reflect the views of the publisher, and the publisher hereby disclaims any responsibility for them.

ISBN: 978-0-595-42383-5 (pbk)
ISBN: 978-0-595-86719-6 (ebk)

Printed in the United States of America

For Riel

.

This book is <u>not</u> a how-to guide for the grieving. It is <u>not</u> an account of grief remembered from the other side. I wrote this while in the clutches of mourning to explore my new reality and to keep a sense of my now-dead son, Sam, close to me. It is a very personal work. I share it to honor his memory and because I believe anyone who's mourning the death of a loved one secretly wants to connect with every aspect of the missing.

Contents

THE END OF ONE LIFE ...

My son, Sam, died while on his dream adventure to Africa. It was his first trip to another continent, an act of courage to prove he could do anything he wanted.

I sent him on his way in late October 2003, proud of his determination but anxious about his being so very far away. In my motherly fantasies after he left, I imagined him losing his passport, being robbed of all his money, or standing surrounded by dozen curious villagers, trying to explain that he needed a doctor. But I kept these images to myself.

Sam quickly formed African roots, volunteering at a day care center in Kumasi, Ghana. The kids loved him, and the other teachers listened to what he, the young white man, had to say. He packed a small bag almost every weekend, riding for hours in cramped buses to see as much of the country as possible. His e-mails came often and were packed with the excitement of a twenty-five-year-old discovering new worlds and ways of living.

During Christmas break, he traveled to the north country, looking for elephants and other animals in the wild. He caught cerebral malaria during the trip but did not get sick until after his return to Kumasi two weeks later. The time from his last "everything's great" e-mail to his death was an astonishingly short seven days.

We did not know anything was wrong until after Sam died. Grief arrived at our doorstep on an ordinary Wednesday morning when detectives, dispatched by the Department of Foreign Affairs, came to give us the news of his death.

From that point onward, my life and the lives of friends and family were thrown into chaos. Such a rip in the fabric of life is not easily mended. Each of us, in our own way and in our own time, had to take the inevitable journey toward understanding and acceptance.

1

During the first few weeks after Sam died, I panicked, afraid that I would forget him. I looked at pictures of him, but I could not hear his voice. I remembered words he would say, but could not conjure up expressions on his face. One night I decided to write him a letter. From the first "Dear Sam," he was there, close to me. From then on, whenever I needed to feel him near, I wrote him another letter.

And so the book began.

After finishing one particular letter, bawling profusely as I typed out the last sentences, I leaned back; I expected the usual relief at having put my guts down on paper. Instead I imagined Sam reading the letter. I could even hear in my head what he would say back if he had the chance. Without thinking, I started writing. The words typed themselves, my fingers moving to the sound of his voice inside my head. I was very aware, writing for him, that this was not exactly the person he was in life. My typing did not capture his goofy spelling. While alive, he occasionally talked about the important things in life, but he was never as comfortable in this area as he comes across in the book. Somehow, in my own mind, the act of dying gave him wisdom about these things, and that perspective helped me to untangle my own confused ramblings.

Wherever they came from, Sam's letters brought him back into my life for a short while, and his words from the other side were a great comfort to me.

I think of this book as the last thing that Sam and I did together.

◆   ◆   ◆

I would like to thank the Quebec Writers Federation for accepting me into their mentorship program. Without my mentor, Elaine Kalman Naves, this book would still be sitting uncompleted in a file on my computer. She gave me deadlines, gently pointed me in directions that were necessary but painful, and gave me the kind of encouragement writers dream of.

I am also grateful to my dearest friends, Sandy and Jared Namenson, who added their invaluable editing skills. I know this task was made even more difficult because of the death of Sandy's own son.

Despite losing Sam, I consider myself a very lucky person. My son Riel is a treasure, and I have a large and loving family and community of friends. I try to count my blessings often and deeply.

Getting this book out of me was not a pleasant exercise. I have often wondered if it was a good thing to march headlong into the pain and explore it rather than allowing it to bubble up on its own accord. But if my book serves as a helping hand to even one person who is gripped by grief, it will have been worth it.

Montreal, 2005

SAM'S STORY

Sam was born at home in March, 1978. He came roaring into the world with the same intense commitment to purpose that he brought to all his plans later in life. My contractions had the force of a Mack truck ramming into a brick wall. They came back-to-back, with no relief in between. From the moment I woke up, wondering if this was really it, until he fell asleep in his cradle for the first time, was just over two hours.

Sammy was a contented baby, as second children often are. While his two-year-old brother, Riel, plotted schemes for getting rid of him, he slept and smiled through each attempt, eventually winning a place in Riel's heart with his quiet charm.

Sammy approached his first few years cautiously, not wanting to undertake anything until he could be sure of success. Each traditional milestone of infancy was accomplished much later than the books predicted. He didn't crawl until eight months, but the minute he started, he was rock-steady on his knees and hands. Sam was well over a year and a half before he began to walk, but his first steps were solid, and he rarely fell after he decided that walking—and running—were good ideas.

Talking was another matter. His father, Lenny, and I offered him the same Montreal bilingual landscape that we had offered Riel: day care in French, English at home. While his brother made a clear distinction between the two languages, hearing and understanding French but speaking only English, Sam tried to mix the two. Sam would choose whichever word, English or French, that he could find in his head to get through a sentence. This strategy soon got him in big trouble. If he started off in English and then added some French, he got caught in sentence-structure hell. Not knowing how to climb out of this quagmire, at age four he stopped talking altogether.

By this time, Lenny and I began to acknowledge that our cute little red-haired Sam was not merely cautious but seriously struggling with each basic skill he tried to learn. We took him to a clinic where, dozens of tests later, the doctors pronounced a diagnosis of aphasia. In a nutshell, aphasia is a kink in the memory hardwiring of the brain. Sam, like all of us, received information and then stored it away in his head's filing cabinets. But he could not retrieve his knowledge; he could not find the correct file drawer for the information he wanted. Only after dozens and dozens of repetitions—from math tables to writing a word, from the name of a vegetable to the name of a person—would he be able to speak a word or offer a math solution when he required it.

Once we knew what Sam was dealing with, we reorganized things to make his life a little easier. We took him out of French day care and made sure he had only one language to learn and wander around in. After a very difficult first year in grade school, we decided to hold him back, and he repeated first grade to get another run at the basics. Tutors and special education teachers were permanent fixtures during his school years. But regardless of the resources we assembled, the world of academics, with its emphasis on testing, memorizing and quick-access answers, remained outside his grasp for his entire life.

But Sam was smarter than most when it came to figuring out what was happening around him. He was totally tuned into the moods and relationships of people he encountered. One day soon after his father and I separated, just before he turned five, he called me on the phone to tell me that "Daddy won't say anything, but I know he's sad. I think you should come back and cheer him up." When my mother died in a car crash, he appointed himself, at the age of eight, as my comforter, sitting on my lap at every opportunity, giving hugs rather than taking them. As he got older, this ability to sense what others were feeling and needing made him a terrific friend and mentor of children.

When Sam turned eleven, his physical challenges kicked in. He started complaining that his legs hurt, and sometimes, when he was trying to get out of the car or get up from the couch, he said they ached so much that he couldn't move them. Lenny and I assumed these were growing pains since Sam was adding an inch to his height every few months. One day, however, the aches took an ugly turn. He and Riel were watching TV in the living room. When I got back from a small food-shopping trip up the street, Riel came to the door to let me in. As I walked toward the couch to say something to Sam, I found him on the floor, unconscious, eyes rolled up into his head, seemingly dying. I started screaming, cradling him in my arms, unable to move away from him even to get help on the phone. Riel took over and called 911, and an ambulance arrived as Sammy was slowly coming back into this world. We had witnessed the end of a grand mal seizure, and he had several more at the hospital until the medication finally took effect. During the next few months, often before falling asleep, he continued to have seizures, though not that often. Finally a combination of medicines held them at bay for the most part.

Sammy had not yet reached adolescence, and the load he was carrying would have crippled many adults. School was one unsuccessful hurdle after another. His daily medication, while keeping his seizures to a minimum, dulled his motor reflexes and speech. But with that unique strength that only a child can bring to adversity, he put his problems on the back burner and focused on the things he enjoyed.

Working his little entrepreneur side, Sam sold his friends twenty-five-cent shots at his Game Boy. He always had several dollar bills in his pocket. Crinkling them as he walked down the street always brought a dreamy smile to his face.

He relished offering up Riel, two years older and better at games and sports, to my disciplinary rage. Out of the blue, lounging on the couch, two rooms away from where Riel was playing quietly, Sam would yell: "Mom, Riel hit me and took away my toys." I rarely questioned the validity of his accusation—it was a routine dynamic in our household. I would march in and berate a surprised Riel, assuming his protestations were just last-ditch attempts to avoid punishment. Riel could see what I couldn't behind my back: a smirky smile and a twinkle in the eye of the real culprit, safe on the sidelines.

When Sam discovered something he liked, he embraced it wholeheartedly. *Alf* was not just his favorite television program; it was a lifestyle that included stuffed animals of various sizes, a key chain, stickers, coloring and reading books, T-shirts, and underpants. *The Dukes of Hazzard* produced miniature jeeps, a lunch box, shirts, headbands and wristbands, and Mr. T-style tests of strength. *90210* required weekly tapings and school binders with the stars' faces stamped on the front covers. Sam was the ideal target for product spin-offs.

One of Sam's biggest loves was sports. I'm sure he would agree with me that he never excelled in any of the games he tried. As a youngster, he could never get his legs straight enough in hockey skates. When he joined the football team, he spent 98 percent of each game on the bench. Wrestling was a little better: he actually made it once to the regional semifinals, but after high school, he was never chosen for a team. Rugby was his real love, but he broke his nose, was scared of getting a head injury, and often experienced seizures from running around the field.

In a world where success is judged by individual achievements, most kids with his skills would have written off athletics. But Sam dedicated himself, over and over again, to finding a role in every sport he undertook. The high school football team gave him an award at their annual ceremony for being the person who brought the best team spirit to the game. In wrestling, he sweated through three levels of coaching exams and eventually became a referee at tournaments in Montreal and Ottawa. As a journalist follows every detail of current events, Sam studied the sports pages and TV game analyses so he would be up on the game chatter. His favorite way to spend an evening was watching a Habs hockey game with "the boys"—a close-knit gang of Riel's friends, who had accepted him into the fold. Until he left for Africa, he was the goalie for pick-up Sunday afternoon street hockey games, one of the few players who never missed a game. He was known affectionately as "Five-Hole Sam" because of his unerring success at stopping every puck flung at him *except* those that flew between his legs.

Sam's teenage years were quite different from those of other boys. His seizures robbed him of getting a driver's license at age sixteen, and even the slightest amount of alcohol in his system would start tremors in his legs. While his friends were taking those first independent steps toward freedom, he was caught in a straitjacket. Always sober and without wheels, he tried chewing tobacco and pot, the former giving him nothing but a sore mouth and bad breath; the latter, a nice high if pure but a severe seizure if cut with anything at all.

Despite my pleas, Sam insisted on keeping his medical condition a secret throughout his teenage years. This strategy often caused even more grief when his friends had to watch, dumbfounded, as he crumpled to the ground with a surprise attack of leg tremors. But nothing I said would convince him to come out of the closet. Looking back, I realize it was his first step toward taking control of his own medical decisions.

Sammy's graduation from high school did not open up a world of possibilities. While everyone he knew was making plans to move on to university or technical school, Sam was caught without a single idea about what to do next. The academic life was impossible, which ruled out any path that required schooling. Sports were his only passion, but he wasn't good enough at any game to turn it into a career. He thought about becoming a physical education teacher, but he wanted out of school, not back in again. His employment options in Montreal were severely limited by his poor grasp of French. To escape the decision about what to do next, he applied for a position as a counselor-in-training at Kamp Kanawana, the place he had spent practically every summer since he was eight, and was accepted.

That summer was terrific. Sam was considered a good counselor with the kids, especially the younger ones, who called him "Daddy" and ran to him whenever a bout of homesickness came over them. He was able to share with them a child's enthusiasm for the outdoors while using a firm, older hand to keep them in line.

However, once camp was over, he was no further ahead with a life plan than before. Our relationship took a real nosedive because I was constantly trying to come up with work ideas, and he was just as constantly rejecting every proposal. He started spending more and more time on the couch in front of the TV. I deposited my ideas for him with close friends in the hope that suggestions from others might carry more weight. But whatever ideas were offered, nothing interested him or seemed feasible.

Finally I bumped into someone whose kid had been wallowing in the same ditch but ended up breaking the cycle by joining Katamavik, a government program for young adults. A quick call revealed that, although the fall session of eight months had just started, there was room for one more kid from Quebec. Katamavik seemed made for Sam: French and English kids were put together to teach one another their languages. Each participant was assessed and placed in community projects as a volunteer. During the eight months of the program, the group would travel to three different parts of Canada—Sam's destinations were Saskatoon, Saskatchewan; northern Ontario; and Tatamacouche, Nova Scotia.

Sammy embraced the idea—especially the part about going away—and transformed himself overnight into a focused ball of energy. Every day he had a list of things to do and tasks to complete. Within a week, he was on his way to Saskatchewan, the spring back in his step, the excitement of new plans re-igniting the sparkle in his eyes.

I think it was during his time with Katamavik that Sam found his calling. His first placement was in an aboriginal school, assisting with first and second graders who almost all came from abusive homes. The kids flocked to him. Big and clumsy, with affection to spare, he became their confidant, their comfort, the "adult" who laughed at their jokes and taught them the joy of sports. He told me once that he preferred working with kids who were fighting uphill battles. Given his own challenges, he understood their behavior and their will to survive.

When Sam arrived back from Katamavik, there was a confidence in him that I had never seen before. He quickly went off to spend another summer as a camp counselor at Kamp Kanawana but told me that when he was finished, he was going to move to Ottawa. He wanted to live on his own, without the family safety blanket, in a place where speaking English was all he had to worry about.

The next few years of Sam's life were a roller-coaster of new and exciting plans followed by the reality of broken dreams. Transplanted to Ottawa, he worked at a vegetable market but had to move home when his seizures started up again and he needed constant care during a change in his medication. He went off tree-planting one summer but lost money because he just couldn't work as quickly as he needed to make a profit. He enrolled in travel agent school with the dream of organizing travel excursions for people with medical difficulties but couldn't handle the academic load. He started taking business courses at Vanier College and wrote a proposal for a Sports Day Care Centre but couldn't find a partner to help with the financial end of things. He got a job washing dishes at a day care and managed to talk the supervisor into letting him set up a sports program for the kids; but money got tight, the sports program was canceled, and he was posted back to washing dishes.

Finally, in the spring of 2003, Sam quit his job at the day care. As he told me, he was tired "of getting the worst jobs because I don't have a degree and dealing with spoiled, middle-class kids." He knew his calling was child care, but he needed to do something special with it.

And he had a plan.

With an even more ferocious focus than usual, he started researching child care jobs in places like India and Africa. He decided to spend the summer again as a counselor at Kamp Kanawana, but he continued making arrangements to leave on a trip in the fall.

Sam's last summer at camp was magnificent for him. He was chosen "Boss Man," the leader of the winning team for the end-of-summer games. His contribution to Kanawana that summer and his talents for mentoring kids brought him a new level of respect and confidence. He fell in love with another counselor and was loved back in that warm and wonderful way that only happens the first time.

Buoyed by his success at the camp and the love of his girlfriend, he came home and tackled his travel plans. Although it often seemed as if the trip would end up as yet another failed dream—most of the programs required a financial contribution that he just didn't have—he refused to give up. He finally found a placement in Ghana that he could afford—not for a year, as originally planned, but for six months or so.

It became clear to me during the planning of his trip that Sam was determined to take control of the direction of his life. Having so often been robbed of plans because of his health or his learning disability, he was taking the reins and surmounting whatever obstacles lay in his path.

Going to Africa, he did accomplish his dream. I just wish it hadn't killed him.

SAM'S E-MAILS FROM AFRICA

Subject: Kumasi, Africa
Date: Wed, 05 Nov 2003 19:27:03 +0000

Hey everyone

It's so hot in africa and you can't get away from it. Right now I'm sitting in a internet place writting on a reall slow computer and its driving me crazy, but anyways.

I'm staing in Kumasi about 4 hours away from Accra the capital city, its a great place to live very beautiful with the palm trees everywhere even in my backyard cool eh. I'm hanging out with vollunteers around the world there all cool and giving me ideas for trips to take when the leave because there term is almost over and I'm taking over for one of them.

I'm living with a family in the daycare very nice and cool work is good I'm teaching 3 kids in a class room but having trouble because the last teacher was strict and scared the kids and there so scared of her so when shes in the room they don't move or talk and I got mad at her today for telling the kids shame on the and I explained your shootin there selesteem down and don't shout at the kidds. Its tough but fun and the school has a cane to smack the kids with and learning I do have the power to take it away and have said thingfs about using the cane on the kids. Things are great just exploring the city of Kumasi actually happy I landed in Kumasi not Accra it didnt seem that great. but happy and the kids are so good and cute they come in uniforms and we change them so they dont get dirty and change them when the day is over. I just work with 3 kids but one is sick so I haven't seen her yet.

I can't explain how hot it is here, another thing when you take a bath they give you a bucket of water with a small pail and then you wash your self like that, So I don't shower every day but its cool you work a system on how to wash your self, another cool thing you walk aroun africa and every thing is on peoples head balancing and sellin everything on the streets. All drinks are usuall you drink things out of bags pretty cool the way you adapt to them and eating there food is really good but makes shit alot I can keep writing all night but Ill save some for next time. I hope everything is good with all.

love you all see yah later. Keep e-mailling me ok

p.s. do you have any tricks on how to stop sweating in hot weather

◆   ◆   ◆

Subject: SAM KUMASI
Date: Thu, 20 Nov 2003 17:20:52 +0000

Hey Guys

how are you? Everythings in Kumasi is great, a nice winter. Sucks to be you in Canada.

I went to a football (soccer) game in the major stadium it was a ok game of Ghana vs Somalia a quarter finals game to get in the wolrd cup games in 2006. Everyone gets in the game and people paint there bodies, but you really notice your the only white person in the stadium, but theses guys I met Prince, Nana and Peter made me at home and are really nice. Ghana won at the end 2-0. People were climbing the fence on to the field just to see the players, I took some pictures.

Now the volunteers left yesterday to Mali, so theres only 2 me and a girl Mollie whos pretty kool but her accent from minneasota is a little annoying but we are traveling buddies. We are traveling to Cape Coast on Friday its suppose to beautiful and theres a park where the Canadians biuld a bridge and looks pretty kool in the pictures I've seen and relaxing on the beach not to rub that in to all of you in the cold weather. See yah later

SAM LAZARUS

◆   ◆   ◆

Subject: Cape Coast Trip
Date: Mon, 24 Nov 2003 17:08:37 +0000

Hey everyone

Friday I left for the Cape Coast, on a tro tro is a van they cram everyone in and not comfy, but very cheap. Its about 4 hours in a tro tro to the cape coast.

The first night we couldn't figure out how to turn the fan on so we had to sleep with no fan and we were sharing a bed. We went to Kakum park and walk on he canopy bridge, Its a brige made of rope that lies high in the rainforest you can see far into the rainforest. After the bridge went to Elmina Fort a big fort made in the late 1400 by the Portuguese was a fort for trading slaves for about 400 years. It's amazing walking through the Fort and learning the history of it and Ghana.

The next day went to Cape Coast castle another slave trading post. They would trade the slaves to Europe, and the states from that casle and others, and theres forts all along the coast of Ghana and the west african countries. After that right back on the packed tro tro (oh I hate them).

Thats my trip this weekend more of a history trip and learned alot about the history of slavery and Ghana.

Now back to teaching in the Daycare.

SAM LAZArus

◆   ◆   ◆

Subject: African weekend
Date: Mon, 01 Dec 2003 17:57:51 +0000

Hey Guys

Not doing much. But had a good week last week except Friday. I got mad at a teacher when I saw her slapp a kids hand and told her no slapping kids and she gave me a lot of adtitude I just ignored her. And the teachers are lazy in the school they don't move until I say and, they've been there longer than me. Thats life in Ghana. I'm realizing that.

I went to a club on Saturday with some volunteers to Foxy Trap it was ok but very expensive. So we ask someone to show us the way to another bar. He was nice and walked with us to the bar about a 20 min walk. It was better bar, with a big terrase and everyone wanted to talk to us because we are white and must be "Rich". Thats there perception of the white men and woman. But ended up to be a good night in the end.

Woke up on Sunday and Kofi took me to a town called Obausi to watch a Football (soccer) game. Before the game Kofi showed me around and a very rich town from the gold mines. Lots of fun watching the game everyone is screaming and gets into the football game but the referee was horrible. Kotoko vs Goldfield 1-Nil.

Then after the game the fights broke out in the stadium. They really love there football team's. Kotoko hasn't won in that stadium in 10 years. Kotoko was happy to win and, break the losing streak in that stadium. Went back home and So much cheering on the side of the road, on they way home.

That is my weekend not much, but different than in Montreal.

See Yah Later.

SAM

◆   ◆   ◆

Subject: African Journey
Date: Tue Jan 6, 2004 12:17:27 PM America/Montreal

Hello Everyone

Before I start telling about my journey, I want to wish a happy Christmas and channuka and a great New year and all and the best to come.

Now the fun starts. I started about 9:00 pm leaving Kumasi heading to Tamale to Northern Ghana (I was travelling alone on this trip). I got in Tamale about 5:00am, and run to the tro tro park to try and find a tro tro to Mole National Parc and the person tells me theres no bus to Mole until 3:00pm. I was upset I just wanted to get there.

I met a old man at a chop bar eating breakfast, who showed me around Tamale on his scooter that was nice of him and after found my self asleep on my bag. Then left for Tamale and on the dirt road where at some points there was no road and looking at the clay huts and little villages and saw how they lived with no electricity and stuff we have and realise how happy we should be.

Finally got their at Mole National Park and ran to my Dormitory room (living as cheap as I can) and got my self settled. Then went to the restraunt and spotted some people who I met in Kumasi and sat down and chatted with them and waited for my meal, and it took about 2 hours and I got mad at them. Thats one thing the service is very slow it could take 1 hour or 2 hours for your food to come.

I slept in and missed the walk in the rainforest in the morning, a little upset but it's ok. I walked in the afternoon and saw all kinds of animals, Antelopes, some crocodiles, some wharthogs (big pigs with tusks), and green and red monkeys and Baboons, who get really close to you, and lots of birds but no elephant a little dissapointed.

I went out the next day early in the morning about six am and saw an elephant. Who wondered into the village, just eating grass a very gentle elephant and then left. Then I was Happy I saw my elephant. A guy I met took his 4 wheel car into the parc and brought me along was fun but only saw 2 monkeys and got fined for driving in the parc but that much. Then relaxed swam in the pool, I left the next day

I woke up to catch my bus at 5am but it never showed up, they told us it was broken sorry. I started to walk with this two girls I met, and ended jumping into a truck with them, and it took us to Damongo and from Damongo I jumped in a big truck carrying something with a tarp over. On that trip we saw a bus roll over into a ditch and I ran to the bus and carried people out of a broken window and check the people for serious injury, but no one was really hurt only scraps. Then are truck stopped at the next village to get more help.

Then the truck drop me off at the junction and then caught a tro tro to Tamale. Took a tro tro to Yendi and from Yendi took a big Truck to Bimbilla and was all covered in red from the sandy road and parts of the way their was no road. Spent the night in Bimbilla.

Then off to Hoe Hoe took a tro tro a long trip it took about 7 hours and got to Hoe hoe. Look around for a phone to call home to say Merry Christmas and Happy Channuka and that I'm alive. I walked around saw the town when some locals took me to a club. The only white man in the club, Lots of fun.

Woke up the next day and headed to the Wli too see beautifull falls and swam in the falls too.

Then to see Togo (french country) so I took a Tro tro too Afalo and walked into Lome. But before I got in it's hard for a white man to get in. The customs officer asks for more money and I said what, but people were telling me just pay so I payed him and saw him put the money in his pocket, and went in. So you see how corrupt the place is before you get in.

When I arrived I went right to the market and saw lots of clothe, food and everything you need. Then off to the Fetish markets and saw dead animals skulls and all kinds of things, they explained voodoo to me and it was very interesting.

After I went out to eat and this guy followed me and sits down with me. I tell him before we order anything "look I'm not going to pay for you" and he says ok and I made sure there was seperate bills but he ran off when I wasn't looking. I had to pay for him, and walked to my hotel mad.

Next day went to the Togo national museum very interesting about the history. After went to my hotel to check out. Then took a motor to the border. At the border I put my bage down to put a book away and the police came to me with hitting canes trying to scare me but it didn't work. Then a police man was calling me, and I kept walking until a person taps my shoulder and I turn around see the policeman and he wanted me to begg on my knees sorry to him because I didn't turn around right away.

I said "sorry" and left Togo

I just went home after Togo I didn't enjoy my stay their and was very tired from my journey.

SAM

◆   ◆   ◆

Date: Tue Jan 6, 2004 12:58:15 PM America/Montreal
Subject: African New Year

Hey Everyone

Happy New Year.

Sorry I'm sending this e-mail one the same day as my trip e-mail I had problems with the computer.

How was everyones New Year?

Mine was very interesting. I decided to go with my family to church and I ended up with huge church service and praying for all my sinns in 2003 and for a better year. But the church was lots of singing and dancing and everyone gets into it so it was ok.

But life stops in Kumasi to pray for all your sinns, no one around not even in the clubs until church was over and then they all go to the clubs. After I was free man with no sinns, but my Kofi (My family's father) did ask me if I would give life to Jesus I said "no not for me" and he respected my answer. I went to Foxtrap bar and danced and played billiard but their rules are very different than ours, and there tables are tiny compared to our pool tables it's funny. The end of the night I ended up with sinns, so I guess next year I'll have to go to church pray for all my sinns again. It's a on going battle of sinns.

That was my New Year it was ok. I wish I could of been with my friends and family.

Oh anyone has news on the Habs please e-mail me please.

I have to go eat dinner. SeeYah

SAM

◆   ◆   ◆

This was the last message we received from Sam. He went into the Komfo Anokye Teaching Hospital with malaria two days later on January 8, 2004. He died at 3:30 in the morning on January 13th.

THE NEWS

January 14

Dear Sam,

I want you to know what happened when we first heard you'd died. It's what I think about most … that day, the arrival of the news, keeps playing over and over through my mind like a slow-mo film on a continuous loop. Without your side of the story, it feels like arriving in the middle of a nightmare—the cause, the most important facts, lost somewhere in a country I do not know and cannot imagine. I give you our story so at least one of us has a complete picture.

Wednesday, January 14, 2004—You are already thirty-six hours gone. Two female cops arrive at our doorstep, carrying a fax from Ghana in their hands. Your brother Riel is home alone to greet them. (Remember when, at age twelve, he had to call 911 when you had your first seizure? Fifteen years later, he steps up to the plate again.)

He buzzes my cell, telling me to come home immediately. He won't say why, and for some reason I don't question his authority. I decide, during the cab ride home, that the bathroom ceiling has collapsed because the neighbors upstairs have taken a particularly long and leaky shower. As I ride up Park Avenue, I'm getting more and more irritated at him for not just going next door to the landlord and demanding that someone come and fix it. For a split second, as I pass the lion statues on Mont Royal Park, I wonder if something has happened to you. But I brush the thought away, scolding myself for having dark and morbid fantasies on such a bright, albeit cold, sunny day.

As I walk in the door, Riel comes down the hallway with a face I have never seen before. There is "something wrong" written in his eyes, but each time he looks at me, he cannot speak.

Two uniformed women appear out of nowhere. What are they doing here? What's Riel done? Is he in trouble with the law?

He finally comes close and looks me dead straight in the eye: "It's Sam."

"What ... Sam?" I ask him. Then I raise my voice, yelling at the ladies: "What about Sam?"

"Il est mort, Madame." He's dead.

A sound comes out of me from some prehistoric tunnel buried deep in the bottom of my stomach. A wail, a groan, a rumbled cry. Eventually it shapes itself into piercing, emphatic words: "NO. NO. NO. NO. NO. NO. NO. NO."

Continuing my mantra, I back haltingly into the front room, away from the policewoman who's trying to hand me a paper.

"Un fax, Madame. Vous devrez le lire, Madame." A fax. I have to read it.

Cornered between the couch and fireplace, I take the fax and try to focus on the words, the letters, the official stamp."Office of Foreign Affairs. Kumasi, Ghana. Samuel Lazarus DECEASED."

Deceased?

I throw the paper at the woman and crumple to the floor as a wave of "Deceased" passes over me. Then another wave. And yet another.

Each wave is followed by a torrent of unbelievable ideas. He died all by himself? What did he die of? Was he sick, or did someone shoot him? Did he really die? How could he have died? Why didn't we know anything? I just heard from him a few days ago, and he sounded fine. Was he sick but didn't tell me? Where did he die? In a house, in a hospital, on the sidewalk?

My mind is racing at the speed of light. There's no space for speech. I keep seeing the word DECEASED jump from the paper. I try to clear it from my mind. It becomes a jumble of letters, then turns into a real word again.

The fantasies of you in Africa and the rhythmic return of the word DECEASED stop only long enough for a new, overwhelming wave of pain to swallow me.

The cops leave.

◆   ◆   ◆

It's so final, Sam. The hardest, most extreme definition of *gone*. No last phone call. No Shake 'N Bake chicken, no Habs games … ever again. No final words. Just a bunch of loose ends and images flapping in the wind.

I see you in the hospital bed, lying very still, very sick, knowing this is the Real Deal: death with a capital D. But not quite aware of what *The End* finally means to you or to the rest of us.

On the other hand …

Perhaps you stared Death in the eye and, realizing your time was up, accepted the verdict and slipped away.

Either way, right now I envy your experience. It seems easier than what I'm going through.

I miss you.

Love, Mom.

◆   ◆   ◆

Dear Mom,

I am so sorry I could not tell you what I was going through before I died. It was very hard being sick with malaria for the first few days. My liver was swollen, so my stomach stuck out, and I hurt all over. I had quite a few seizures in my legs, but only because I was too weak to keep them from happening.

When the doctors started the medicine, I got much better very quickly. Koffi and Tina, the people I was staying with, were very good and came to see me every day. They brought me food—though it was not really what I wanted to eat—and watched over me.

I was ready to go home on Sunday, but the doctors decided to keep me one more night, and that's when the real sickness hit. For the most part, I was in a coma—a black space where you sort of float through nothing. Sometimes you can hear what's going on in the real world, but it is very far away, and you can't say or do anything to show you are aware of things. Sometimes I came back to earth for a brief period of time. Once I saw that Koffi was with me. He looked very worried and upset, but I gave him the thumbs up so he would know I was really OK.

At some point, I knew I was going to die. You were right about that. But it was not a horrible thought. Not like those times when I was younger and had just gone through a grand mal seizure. When those were over, I wanted to die because I didn't want to go through another one. This was different. It was like my whole body was moving toward death, and it seemed like a perfectly natural place to go.

I thought about all of you while I was dying. Images of you, Dad, Riel, Marlene, Patrick, and Rochelle would come into my mind … family dinners, spooning on the couch, watching the Ed show, hockey games, Christmas mornings, playing cribbage … each image came wrapped in love. I didn't think about leaving you or never seeing you again. It wasn't like that. It was more like you all were with me, and I was taking you wherever I was going.

I'm sorry it's so tough for you.

Your son, Sam

After Midnight ...

I try to calm my mind so I can slip into sleep, but I am scared to close my eyes. The darkness is limitless, the perfect setting for a cascade of memories, each one striking at my heart.

I have lost complete control of my mind. Images come flying toward me, each one scaring me with its surprise attack and random arrival: Sam is lying on a hospital bed, crying and feeling abandoned. Sam is in a coma, oblivious to everything around him. With Koffi holding him, Sam is trying to walk out the door of his house in Africa, his stomach extended, his legs buckling with tremors. The doctors are pulling a sheet over Sam right after he has died. Doctors and nurses heave his body into a coffin. To wipe away the images, I plead for Sam to come into my dreams, to tell me what's going on, to tell me good-bye, to tell me everything is OK. Let him come. Let him come. Let him come.

THE BEREAVEMENT BASH

January 15-19

Sammy,

As soon as people started hearing that you had died, they came to the house. Devastated, my best friend and your half-sister/half-mother, Shirley, could not stay home alone. Auntie Mickey called from California, announcing she was leaving for Montreal in the morning. Lenny and Marlene had to be with me, and I had to be with them ... so they came over as well. Riel camped out in his room most of the time, writing fervently, as if his own life depended on the number of pages he filled with details about you. Mike came over, and so did Sheila, Judy, Victor, Josh, and Harry. Before we knew it, the house was full of people and food.

I did not want a party. But when the others weren't there, an eerie quality filled the place, as if my house was haunted with something other than ghosts. We could do nothing on our own but pace. Riel and I would walk up and down the hallway, sometimes together, sometimes in opposite directions. There was nothing to do, nowhere to go. The real world had disappeared, and a new world, filled with death and silence, had taken over our lives. Every once in a while, one of us would break down, and the other would hold on. Then the pacing would begin again.

So the party was preferable.

I didn't quite understand why all the people were coming. Not just close friends, although they would have filled the house. But others we barely know. Workers from your day care. Campers from Kanawana. People from Galafilm. Old friends we had not seen in years.

Although I didn't know it at the time, they had to come for themselves. Someone finally told me that you were the first of our children to die, and then I understood. I could almost hear each one chanting softly: "There, but for the grace of God, go I."

During the five-day Bereavement Bash, we had a routine. Your dad and Marlene would wake up at their place around 4:30 or 5 AM and go straight to their photo albums. They would look at pictures of you, sobbing, and remembering. The kids, Patrick and Rochelle, would wake up later, eat breakfast silently, and then go to school in a daze.

I would get up at my end of town, hit upside the head again with the news. In a grieving, sleepy trance, I would make coffee and stare at nothing for what might be a few minutes or an hour. Variations of *How can it be?* rolled over my mind and took me nowhere and everywhere at the same time.

Perhaps I would shower, perhaps not. For some unexplainable reason, I could not wear jewelry. It was impractical to use makeup because of all the crying and carrying on. I threw on warm, fuzzy fleeces because they felt good when I hugged myself and wailed.

Around ten in the morning, your dad and Marlene would come over to my house. We would try to focus on making the calls that would get your body home from Africa. Even though someone was always breaking down, remembering something about you, we managed to keep in touch with Odette at Foreign Affairs to follow the progress of your trip back to Montreal.

Around noon, Shirley would arrive. She took on the thankless task of informing everyone about what had happened. You can imagine what that was like.

"Hi. Is Ted there?"

"Ted, I've called with some very bad news. Sammy died in Africa … Ted?"

On and on it would go. I think she called more than fifty people. Every once in a while, she got lucky and phoned someone who already knew. Once she finished telling people, she and my friend Sheila took shifts just answering the phone. It rang constantly, about once every fifteen minutes, for days on end.

The steady stream of visitors began around two every afternoon. Sometimes I greeted them. Sometimes I stayed in my room. They brought food and booze and flowers. They talked. They cried. They cleaned the kitchen. We had so many quiches piled up in the pantry that Riel named it "The Leaning Tower of Quiches." Soup was by far the gift of choice ... and it made sense, as it was hot and soothing, except that none of us could eat.

Riel and your buddies—the boys—came over every night, and Josh Plau flew in from Vancouver. I saw that they were scared, but I couldn't mother them as I usually do. I'm sure they were wondering how you, a couple of years younger, had the courage to die. They spoke about you with reverence: it seemed a good attitude to hold onto.

Around four every afternoon, Lenny and Marlene would go home to be there when the kids got home from school. Their place, at the other end of town, would also fill up with family and friends after dinner. Some left early to drive over to my place.

Our homes became gathering places for anyone who needed up-close evidence of the truth: Sammy, about whom Lenny or I had just recently been bragging, had died on his dream trip to Africa. *Died? Are you sure?*

Around 11:30 or so, people began drifting home. Each night, one person would stay longer. The Lingering One. We would go to bed, and the Lingering One would let himself or herself out, ever so quiet and sad.

I camped on the couch because I couldn't sleep in my room. During the day, I went to my room often to grab a smoke or just be by myself. It was comforting as a getaway, but I couldn't sleep there. I guess I didn't want even one little thing to be normal. It was hard enough to take a shower.

Riel was always excited to go to bed. He was sure you would come to him in a dream, and he needed to see you so badly. I slept the dreamless sleep of someone so exhausted that she plunges, instead of drifts, into unconsciousness.

And then came another day, once again bringing the shock: you were gone, and the party would start all over again.

But it didn't change anything. Anything at all.

Mom

After Midnight ...

I can hear the murmur of voices at the table just a few feet away. They soothe me. They're here for Sam and talking about him, most likely, although I can't hear any words. How did I get here? Only a few days ago, everything was normal. I can't remember how that feels. This dream state has become my reality, my surreality. I wonder how long it will last ... or will it ever go away?

I think Sam can see and feel all this. That is what I believe. But it's probably some hollow thought I've manufactured because he is so absent. There's not a trace of him anywhere. He is definitely not in the house. He does not come to Riel or to me in our dreams. I know he is dead, but where is his spirit? Why is he not here with us? Are my beliefs about spirit all wrong?

I should make a to-do list for tomorrow, but every time I do, I can't seem to find or follow it. Tomorrow will be like all the other days since Sam died: a slow, meandering crawl through the hours of the day, going nowhere. What good is a list, after all?

BRINGING YOUR BODY HOME

January 14-24

Dear Sam,

For someone who hated bureaucracy so much (filling out application forms and standing in line drove you to distraction), you certainly managed to create mounds and mounds of red tape by dying in Africa. I guess when you think about it—but who ever does?—it's no surprise that bringing a body home from foreign soil should be a complicated web of paperwork and regulations involving dozens of professionals on three continents.

The first sign that things weren't going to be simple came the day after you died. Odette, the person in charge of your file at Foreign Affairs in Ottawa, told me it might be as long as two weeks before you actually reached Canadian soil. That bit of news sent me into a complete tailspin.

I imagined your body pushed aside, lying covered, on a table in the hospital hallway, waiting for a coroner from Accra to arrive and declare you dead. Did people just pass you by as they went from one hospital task to another? Were they doing anything to protect your body from the heat? Was there a real morgue in Kumasi, or was the village too small to have such a facility?

The answers to these questions became very important to me. I asked Odette, but she didn't know. I felt a little foolish about putting so much emphasis on something that was only a symbol at this point, but your body was all I had left of you.

I realized that I expected things to happen in a certain sequence: hear the news, see the body, have the service, then bury the corpse. In my mind, that was the way it should unfold. The delay in getting your body back turned everything upside down, and no matter how hard I tried to rear-range things in my head, I couldn't see us having a service while your body remained in Africa.

To make matters worse, Odette constantly reminded us that her esti-mate of two weeks was only that: an estimate. Sometimes the process was shorter, sometimes longer. There was no way of telling.

I swear, Sam, this was the most infuriating piece of bureaucracy I have ever had to handle. The reasons for delay just made me want to scream.

The Coroner (or Master Cremator, as he is called there) had to travel from Accra to Kumasi, a six-hour drive, and the earliest he could leave was Friday morning. But everything closes down in Ghana on Friday at noon for the weekend, so even if he left on Friday, he couldn't do anything but wait around until Monday. To spend the weekend with his family, he decided to leave on Monday morning, arrive late in the afternoon, and begin the examination and paperwork on Tuesday—a full week after you had died. His actual work would take only a day, provided you did not have any infectious diseases. If any diseases were found, they would have to be neutralized before the body could be sent to Accra, and this would add another couple of days to the time line. If all went well, you would be on your way to Accra late Tuesday or early Wednesday morning. Koffi agreed to drive the Coroner and you back to Accra, which I imagine was very dif-ficult for him.

International regulations regarding the transportation of bodies across borders require embalming before travel. There were no facilities for this procedure in Kumasi, so the Master Cremator arranged for it to be done in Accra—adding another two to three days, bringing us to Thursday or Fri-day.

With no hitches and no diseases, you could be ready for the airport on Friday evening, in time for the 11:30 flight to London. But this was the best-case scenario. Any deviation from the plan—a traffic jam, a line-up in the morgue, problems with the paperwork—and you would be stuck in the Accra baggage building until the next flight to London on Sunday evening.

The powerlessness of sitting in Canada, thousands of miles away, while each step of this process unfolded, was agony. I considered getting on a plane and arriving in Kumasi to make sure that everyone did their jobs on time but was told it wouldn't make things go any faster (and, in fact, my meddling would probably slow things down). But at various times, I thought I would go nuts just waiting and waiting and waiting to hear what step had been taken or stalled.

Odette, bless her heart, showed the patience of Job with me. Every day I called her, wanting news of where things stood, what had been accomplished, and what came next. If she told me that it looked like the embalming would start around three that afternoon, I called her at three-thirty to make sure someone was there doing it. Without a trace of irritation in her voice, she would agree to find out. She would call Marie at the embassy in Accra, and Marie would in turn call the hospital to see if the embalming had started. Then, through a reverse set of phone calls, the news would roll back to Odette, and she would call me with the latest update. She probably had to handle a dozen files in her docket, but she always gave me the impression that we were the only case she had.

At some point during this regulatory rigamarole, Lenny and I decided to make plans for the service. Things seemed to be going well on the African front, and people here were asking about a funeral date. More importantly, both of us needed to see an end to this purgatory of waiting. Although Odette had said that the earliest you would get into Montreal would be Saturday night, we decided to hang our hopes on that scenario, and we planned the service for Sunday afternoon.

On Friday afternoon, Odette finally called us to say that you were on your way to London. They had managed to get you on that 11:30 evening flight, and you would be arriving there at 6:45 the following morning, London time. Once I stopped worrying about whether you would actually be on the plane, I got upset that you were probably shoved into the baggage compartment. I know, I know … it didn't matter, but I still couldn't separate your body from your person. In my mind, someone should have been sitting with you, a hand on the coffin, for the entire trip.

When we woke up on Saturday morning and checked in with Odette, we found out that a snag had occurred. As the international hub for all such cargo, the London airport has a special location through which all bodies must pass before being sent home. This transit center has a policy requiring a minimum of eight hours from the arrival of the body until the destination flight to allow enough time for checking paperwork and getting the body onto the proper flight. Although the ticket bought for you allowed for eight hours and forty-five minutes, you evidently arrived a little late, and the personnel there decided you would have to stick around for the next flight (Sunday) so that the policy could be respected.

By the time I heard this news, you had been sitting in the hangar for over five hours, and I had less than two hours to get you on the three-thirty plane to Montreal. I became obsessed with this mission. I absolutely would not allow a brief delay and a stupid policy to hold up your trip home.

This challenge became the single most important thing I ever had to do for you. The battle was particularly sweet for me because, as I gathered my journalistic contacts for the assault, I was constantly reminded of how much you loved it when I took on the system—with my complaint letters or phone calls or airtight reasoning with a manager. This was my last such act for you, and I was determined to succeed.

Our friend Melanie and I started contacting British Airways and Irwin Cotler, the Canadian Minister of Justice. With each step up the hierarchies of the civil service and the airline company, we encountered people who could not change things themselves. However, when they heard our story, they ushered us on to someone else who might have more power. The PR woman at British Airways even cleared her agenda for the next few hours to track down a decision-maker who might be able to help.

Finally, just before takeoff time, Mr. Cotler was pulled out of a meeting in Winnipeg. He opened his cell phone and organized a three-way conversation with the head of British Airways and someone in Washington who was in charge of international body transport regulations. All it took was a decision by these guys and a special note in your file on the computer screen. Once that was done, you were released and on your way home.

I thought you would particularly like the three-way cell phone call. I know it didn't make much difference to you, wherever you were in spirit, but it lifted my own mood for a moment to know that you would have appreciated the overriding of a regulation on your behalf.

Mom

◆   ◆   ◆

You're right, Mom. I can't think of anything better than to have some stupid rules changed for me as a parting shot. Just like that time you got us both free tickets from the airline that lost me when I was nine because I walked off the plane in Columbus, Ohio, instead of waiting to land in Dayton, the final stop. Then you were scared. This time you were outraged. Regardless, I have always been proud when you tackle a bit of stupidity and either get it changed or get an apology and an agreement that something makes no sense.

On the other hand, whatever baggage compartment, truck, or hangar I was sitting in didn't make a difference to me. You battled that one for yourself.

Sammy

A VERY CAREFUL TIME

January 20

Sammy,

It's odd, but in the middle of all this shock and pain, I sometimes fantasize about how things could be worse. I could be alone with no friends and no community. I could have no other son, and your death would mean the end of my mothering. Your father and I could be fighting, and Marlene and I could be competing for attention as grieving mothers. Friends could be telling us what kind of service would be appropriate. You and I could have had a fight the last time we spoke.

It might seem like a useless exercise, but these "what ifs" always make me feel lucky somehow. So I go there when things seem particularly dark.

Lenny and Marlene and I have been so careful with each other. Every time one of us makes a suggestion, it is quickly followed by "What do you think? Would you feel comfortable with that?" We seem to be keenly aware of needing each other in order to get through this, and so we avoid any comment that might be judgmental or critical. For instance, not a word is uttered about people smoking in my flat (now is not the time to quit) or which of our friends are dealing with phone calls and service arrangements.

Your Grandpa Herman is devastated. He had just gotten over a very bad bout of pneumonia when I first called him about the news. But your death has made him ill again, and he gets dizzy spells now whenever he walks. Then he got very anxious about the frigid weather here, remembered the stairs up to our apartment, and fretted that the plane ride might make him even sicker. He finally called me, weeping, to say he just couldn't come up for the service.

As you know, he is not much of a talker, so when he said how important it was to be there for me and how horrible he felt about not coming, I was very moved by his open emotion.

The last time I cried with my father was when Mom died, and I have to admit that it was not easy to hear him so vulnerable and sad. He loved you immensely. Thank goodness your Auntie Judy suggested that he come up later when we scatter your ashes (I hadn't even thought of that). When I called him back and told him we would save the cremation service until he could make it, I could sense some of the illness leaving his body. He wanted a last connection with you, and I am glad we can give it to him later.

In your honor, we are looking out for each other in ways we've never done before. Lenny and Marlene and I are connecting as only parents can. Your grandfather and I are feeling the father-daughter bond that has been dormant for many years.

I hate the fact that it was your death that brought us closer, but I can't think of anything else that would have done it.

Mom

◆   ◆   ◆

Dear Ma,

It's hard to see the pain and suffering you're all going through, and know that I'm the cause of it. Such sadness I feel from all of you. And there is nothing I can do to help. So those little acts of tenderness among you, Lenny and Marlene, Grandpa's loving tears for both of us ... these make me feel proud of you all.

Can I be proud? Is that possible now? Along with you, I am also learning about this new reality.

Sam

THE SERVICE

January 25

Samboni,

In the midst of all the people, negotiations to get your body home, and the fact that we're walking zombies, we have to pull ourselves together to plan a memorial service for you. I can't imagine turning myself into an event planner, but it has to be done. Friends are calling from all over, wanting to know when and where the service will be. It's a ritual we owe ourselves, you, and everyone who's hurting.

So Lenny, Riel, Marlene, and I start talking about what we want to do, how to create something that you'd be pleased with. A few things are certain: it has to take place in the neighborhood, the Plateau, your stomping ground. There will be no religious overtones—we never heard a peep from you about religion. And it has to be a grand affair. (Riel told us of a conversation the two of you had after Cousin Drew's funeral service, where twelve hundred people showed up; you both agreed: "We've got a lot of work to do if we want that many people at our funerals.").

On the one hand, it feels good to have some concrete tasks in front of us—a reason to shower, brush our teeth, and put on clean clothes. On the other hand, we're the worst people to do any decision-making right now: we're unfocused, likely to cry if the location is not what we want, prone to forgetting phone numbers and contact names, and not at all interested in what things cost. (It does occur to me, in a callous moment, that I could make a bundle organizing memorial services for people crumpled with grief.)

We pick a date—Sunday, January 25—and put out the word to anyone calling or coming by the house that we need a venue. When suggestions start rolling in, Lenny, Riel, and I turn ourselves into a scouting team.

We have no clear vision of what we want, just an optimistic hope that we'll know the right place when we see it. Are we to pick some place where you might have gone while alive? Or should we try to imagine a conversation we never had, in which you tell us what kind of funeral you want? We kick ourselves for not knowing but can't think of a single time when the topic came up.

So we trek off to places suggested by friends who've recently been to services they liked. There's a trendy, ultramodern funeral home on St. Laurent, with tall avant-garde statues of the Virgin Mary and Jesus. Every third person would have to look around a post there, it costs a fortune, and the guys who run the place give out condolences like candy mints at a restaurant cash register. I try to imagine each one of them with some quirky background like the characters from *Six Feet Under*, but they are just entrepreneurs trying to make a designer buck. Nothing there speaks to us of you.

The next stop is Sala Rosa, the Spanish restaurant-cum-party hall, where Galafilm holds Christmas parties. The atmosphere is much better, and Riel tells us you came here a couple of times for an evening with him and your gang of friends, the boys. We walk upstairs and look at the big empty hall with a stage. There's a funkiness about the place, and I can imagine the dark, bar-drinking feeling sliding away for a sad crowd of young mourners. But it holds only 250 people, and when Lenny, Riel, and I do a quick count of friends and family, we're over three hundred before we know it. We look around to see where an overflow crowd would end up: down the stairs and out into the forty-below frozen street. So we're on our way again.

Our last stop is the old Rialto Theatre, just down the road from our place on Park Avenue. The exterior is like a rundown set from *The Last Picture Show*. Standing outside while waiting for the manager, I imagine latecomers stepping over the early birds who occupy the torn-up seats, maneuvering through popcorn containers still on the floor from better times, in the 1960s. But with no other options, we all hold back our panic as we finally walk through the doors.

The movie seats have been removed, and there is now a polished wooden floor that can accommodate 300-400 chairs. The balcony seats another 500 if needed. There's a beautiful stage with all the art deco trimmings. Two bars on the periphery give the space a festive feeling. We find out that the space is available, and the price is right.

An added attraction you'll appreciate: it's next door to Zorba's souvlaki joint, your absolute favorite place to eat. When the service is over, people can go there for a drink or chat, welcomed by the owners, who are themselves grieving over your death. (When I told them, the two women started wailing, and the two guys kept saying, over and over, "No, that can't be.")

This is the place. We all know it in our hearts.

Once the venue is chosen, the next round of demands must be tackled. People have to be told, chairs have to be rented, speakers chosen, music, flowers, etc., etc. Meanwhile, your mother, the queen of organizers, is out of commission. I can barely remember to take my vitamins, let alone pull together an important event. Yet I can't bear to leave it to anyone else. The whole thing has to be perfect, completely perfect, for you.

Along with sadness and loss and the unreality of it all, I now feel overwhelmed by all the work that has to be done. Finally I stop and give myself a lecture in the firmest voice I can muster: "Grief will have to take a backseat for a few days. Sam deserves the best, so we will have to pull it together. That's it, that's all. Stop weeping and start delegating."

As if in a scene from *Star Trek*, I beam myself into a calm, almost robotic state. I put Shirley in charge of the program, Mickey in charge of flowers, the Galafilm girls in charge of chairs and space set-up. I move the computer into my bedroom, close the door, and pray that you will help me find the words I need to give you an elegant good-bye.

The morning of the service, I awake feeling nauseated. I see flashes of other funerals where grieving parents, children, or spouses have to be dragged down the aisle into their seats. I put myself in their places and feel the same heaviness of heart, rubbery legs, and strong refusal to say a public good-bye. I am scared that the ceremony will be too sad, that all the speakers will paint you as a saint and not as the person we are going to miss. I worry that only a few people will show up because it's one of the coldest days of the year, forty below zero without the windchill.

I try to picture myself on the stage and giving the eulogy, but the image makes the nausea worse. I force myself to read the eulogy out loud again to see if I can get through it without crumpling into tears. After fifteen practice readings, I can make it to the end—but the final good-bye still brings with it a fresh flood of sadness that nearly breaks me in two. I remind myself that crying at the funeral is OK—I am your mother, after all.

Your body is over at Paperman's Funeral Home, having arrived late last night, and I wonder if we should change our minds and bring you into the hall. I know you're not in that shell, but I can't feel you anywhere else. I wonder if you'll show up for your last big event on earth.

My family has arrived from the States and is combing the house for warm clothes to protect them from a bitterly cold day, temperatures they have never before experienced. Ariane, your girlfriend, has taken a bus from Quebec City and arrives at the house at my invitation. I cannot imagine her suffering, her first love cut tragically short. I am aware of all these things, but they are played out in a distant, parallel universe that I cannot reach. I force myself to pull Ariane close to me as we leave, figuring that eighteen years is hardly enough time to prepare for something like this.

As we walk the four blocks to the Rialto, time seems to stop. This trip could be taking five minutes or fifty and I have no sense that I'll ever arrive. The ice-cold wind forces us to fold in on ourselves, and we are all hugging ourselves for warmth. At St. Viateur Street, we are joined by others coming from their homes in the neighborhood. Each greeting is awkward—the first few words are uttered, then stopped as if talking were an embarrassment, unsuited for the occasion. We are glad to see each other but try not to smile.

By the time we arrive, there are a good dozen of us making our way to the doors, a small parade of people who pause before entering, reluctant to go in but anxious to leave the biting cold.

The minute I enter the theatre, I can tell something special is about to occur. There are hundreds of people warming the place with their energy. Old friends meet up with each other; new connections are made among strangers who share their stories of you. Counselors and kids from Kamp Kanawana are everywhere, many at their first funeral. I can see the shock on their young, innocent faces as they gaze at the large poster photograph of you that's been mounted on the stage. I give another small, desperate prayer that your spirit is in attendance, if only from the heavenly bleachers.

I make my way through the crowd, acknowledging each person as I see him or her. Everyone offers a deep hug, often accompanied by tears. I take in the strength from their bodies and give back my own sympathy for their pain and shock. I finally make it to a chair in the front, my legs a little wobbly, and continue greeting those who seek me out. There are not many words exchanged. Funerals are a time for the eyes to speak to each other.

Once in a while, before the ceremony starts, I am left alone for a short time. I absorb the atmosphere, which is unlike anything I have ever felt. A deep blanket of sadness, shaded with the tragedy of a young life cut short, hangs over the room. At the same time, I can feel the intense closeness of a community gathered for a single purpose: to mourn your passing, Sam. Amidst all the weeping and mourning, there is love.

The service unfolds, a surprise to everyone who watches and participates. Each presentation, from different facets of your life, reminds us of who you were and what we have to remember in the days, months, and years to come. Friend, brother, son, wrestler, traveler, camp counselor, colleague, cousin, nephew, student, boyfriend. Everyone's knowledge of you expands to include aspects of your life he or she knew nothing about.

I sit front-row-center, a confusion of emotions whirling around me, surprised that I can take it all in. You are my son, but my sense of you seems suddenly so small, so incomplete. I had no idea how important you were to the kids and the other counselors at Kamp Kanawana—I just helped you pack and washed your clothes at the end of each session. I didn't know you held your cousins' faces down in the snow or taught them how to fart. Your Auntie Ros says you stopped by her house every day, when you were little, on your way home from school. I realized that I never knew your routine when you were staying at your dad's. Anecdote after anecdote, story after story, uncovers someone who was so much more than I thought. While part of me marvels at how deeply you left your mark on this world, another part feels inadequate, ignorant, a poor excuse for the person who is supposed to know you best. I experience my first regret that I did not pay more attention to your life as you were living it.

As my own time to speak approaches, I am gripped by fear. How the hell am I going to make it up the stairs on legs that won't work and speak from a podium with a voice that's probably shut down? The bits of the eulogy I can remember in my head sound silly and trite. If I drone through it, even the good parts will be missed, and I will have let you down.

Shirley calls my name to begin the eulogy.

I walk to the stairs, knowing I have only one chance to do this right. From the podium, I look over the entire crowd—hundreds in chairs and standing on the ground floor; the balcony filled to bursting with camp kids. I take a sip of water before I begin and spot some faces of family and friends. I feel their comfort and love, and I realize that there's not one stranger in the entire place.

I deliver my final words to you with all my love. Grace automatically appears because you deserve the best. A last poem, some African music, and our ceremony is over … and perfect.

We are all surprised at what we have just been through. People who came to support your father and me, people who didn't know you very well, tell us they are sorry they didn't have more time with you. Others say they have never been to such a moving service, and all funerals should be like this one. They all agree that they are leaving feeling better than when they arrived.

I know the service was mostly for those of us left behind. But I hope you can take the essence of it on your next journey.

Good-bye, my sweet child.

Mom

◆　　◆　　◆

Poems for Sam, written by his brother Riel and read at the service:

ON THE ROAD TO KUMASI

On a road in Kumasi, far, far from home,
Walks a man with crooked feet, a carrot top, and smile.
The horizon that glows, long and narrow,
Shines a path through the trees, to destinations unknown.
"Hike on, my good man," cry the birds with their chirps,
"You'll soon meet your maker, hike on toward the light."
Where the path turns left, you take a right,
When the sun falls asleep, the moon is in sight.
Go, man, go, to the end of your quest,
Under African skies lies a chair for your rest.

LIVING PRESENCE

At the farthest far reaches,
Where the land meets the sky,
In the deepest, dark waters,
In the squint of an eye,
On a long, knobby branch,
At the bottom of a soup pot.
Standing on a roof top,
With wind whistling past.
On a rusted park bench,
In the city of our youth,
Under a fingernail,
Under your nose,
Over the fence,
Lost in a rose.
In a storefront display,

Wrapped in ribbons and bows.
In the words of an orator,
In the dreams of a dreamer,
With a hand in the cookie jar,

With a foot at the door,
With an appetite unquenchable,
For what life has in store.
Where the spoke meets the rim,
In the grease on the gear,
When the clock strikes four, or seven,
or nine, or eleven.

On a tro-tro headed northward,
In the thoughts of young children,
By the breast of a butterfly,
On the back of an elephant,
In the sun and the moon and the stars,
In the earth where the worms slither.
At the foot of two beds, two mothers,
In the heart of one father,
In the whims of three siblings.
On the lips of those who love and remember,
Who cherish times past,
Who can recall the sounds,
The smells,
The taste of his cheek.
Under a dark, woolen cap,
In the lining of your coat,
Pulled out of a pocket, put back in,
On the lake in a boat.
Nestled under lily pads,
Ready to pounce.
On a long, wooden pier,
Headed out, but quite near,
Under a glowing, grey sky,
With salvation yet achieved,
Is a dear, delicate spirit,
Who shall never, ever leave,
Our living presence.
Sam.

YOUR CORPSE

January 26

Sammy,

I've been putting off writing to you about your corpse because…. Well, you remember how you freaked out seeing Cousin Drew in the box. Take that experience times a thousand. And as hard as it was to see you there, it feels just as painful to describe it to you.

Your father, while insistent on seeing you one last time, was also very clear it was a personal decision. "There's no right or wrong behavior here. Everyone has to go or not go for themselves." I agreed with his approach: people grieve in different ways, and seeing a corpse is sometimes helpful and sometimes not.

Like Lenny, I was resolved to look at your corpse. I needed to verify that you had really died. I was dreading the actual sight, but only a corpse could convince me this had happened to you.

As I said, your body arrived the night before the service, but Lenny and I decided we would wait to see you. I know, I know. I fought a whole government battle to get you here on time for the service, and now we were keeping you at Paperman's until Monday. But Lenny and I realized, after you arrived, that we could handle only one important marker per day: Thursday, find a venue; Friday, write the eulogy; Saturday, plan the service; Sunday, hold the service; Monday, see the body. We were just not capable of more than that.

Before leaving on Monday morning, I tried to fortify myself with various images of what I thought you might look like: peaceful, chalky, bloated, hollow-cheeked. Every dead body I'd seen in real life or on *Six*

Feet Under appeared before my mind's eye, and I tried to change each one into you. It was a sick little exercise and did nothing to soften the reality.

We arrived at Paperman's Funeral Home—Lenny, Marlene, Riel, and I—and were first ushered into the director's office to do some paperwork. I guess the funeral experts think of paperwork as a kind of Valium for the survivors.

"Here, sign this … and this … and this."

"Here's a plasticized copy of the obit you can have for safekeeping."

"Here's a white manila envelope with our logo on the front to put everything in."

"Now, doesn't that feel better?"

No. Absolutely not. All it did was take me away from the task at hand, and I felt my resolve starting to waver as the minutes ticked away.

Finally, forms and contracts in hand, we were led to a large room with nothing in it but a few chairs and some big pieces of furniture. I was hugging myself for dear life, trying to keep the shakes to a minimum, and concentrating on my feet, which I willed to move one in front of the other. I was very spaced out, even having trouble orienting myself. I expected to arrive in a small room with an open casket as the main feature. This place was empty; it could have held fifty people. There was nothing around except a couple of couches along the wall and a young man standing next to a large decorative table. I thought we had made a wrong turn.

I closed my eyes, shook my head, and then tried to see differently. Oh, yes, on the table is a casket, very African in style, decorated with burnt-wood designs all along the sides and top. I took a brief second to thank Koffi for sending you home in such a lovely box.

As Lenny approached, the man bent down and opened the lid. All my resolve to see you fled instantly. I hovered near the door, miles away, eyes hard shut, backing up against the wall as if the casket contained a bomb. From twenty feet away, I slowly opened my eyes and saw the tip of your nose and a small patch of your forehead. I was sure I was going to vomit.

Pulling myself together, I walked up to the casket to take a good, hard look at you. What I saw only made matters worse. Your face was compressed, your forehead wrinkled down towards your eyebrows, your head turned at a strange angle. It took me a moment to realize that the casket was about five inches too small, so the people at the morgue had been forced to cram you in. I let out a wail and walked quickly away, collapsing onto a couch at the back of the room.

As I cried, I kept thinking: "This is not what I expected. I wanted to see a perfect you." Then, understanding that anything not alive must fall short of perfect, I wailed some more.

Seated on the couch, rocking back and forth, I stopped crying from time to time to catch a wide shot of you across the room. Your left ear was surrounded by hair longer than the #2 buzzcut you usually had. I saw a piece of your jaw with a slight growth of beard. I remembered hearing somewhere that hair keeps growing for a while after a person dies. I did some math: you've been dead for twelve days, and you have about three days' growth on your face. When did you last shave? When was your last haircut? How long had your hair kept growing? I wanted to know these things.

My questions brought me back to my senses, and I forced myself off the couch. I had come to make sure you were dead, and all I had done so far was take a quick look and run away. I had to touch you, to feel your lifeless body, to be sure.

I walked back to the casket and stood over you. You had a very slight smile on your face. You were wrapped from neck to ankles in a piece of plain white muslin. Your feet were propped up against the end of the coffin, and I recognized your toes, although they seemed thinner than when I last saw them sticking out of your sandals.

I looked back at your face and very slowly moved my hand toward your cheek. With every ounce of strength I could find, I finally touched you. There was no warmth. You were not there.

Mom

◆   ◆   ◆

After Midnight ...

I can't sleep. The image of Sam's squashed face has replaced all other visions in my head. I try to concentrate on his feet and toes instead. They are what I want to remember from my time in the casket room. But I can only hold onto them for a few seconds at a time, and then his face comes back to haunt me.

I remind myself it's not my Sammy crammed into that box, but an empty casing, the last vestige of his life on earth. It's the shell's face that was forced into the box with a shoehorn. I focus on the cold feeling of his cheek to keep this thought with me. I imagine his body on a long wooden plank as it is slipped into the furnace for cremation. I have no problem with that ... I do not see it as my son being burned.

But his face, rammed up against the side of the box, keeps coming back, and its distortion will not stop tearing at my heart.

CRYING, PART I

January

Sammy,

Not counting welling up during sad movies, I had not really cried in almost fifteen years. And now I don't think I'll ever stop. It always comes at the end of a big wave of sadness or after a rush of missing you. I'll be fixing some breakfast or stirring my coffee, and suddenly, out of nowhere, I get kicked in the gut with the unbelievable news that you are gone. The minute the news hits, my eyes turn into fountains, great waves of tears to match the waves of shock washing over me. Sometimes the feelings and tears are so intense that I crumple right where I'm standing, falling like a damp rag to the floor. I never knew feelings could cause your legs to buckle.

I've absolutely no interest in how I look, but even if I did, I wouldn't be able to wear makeup. My eyes are puffy and sting relentlessly. The never-ending streams of tears on my face and mouth have caused my lips to chap: painful splits and white crusts have appeared at the corners of my mouth. I have to carry a pot of lip balm wherever I go. I am, in a word, most unappealing. But then again, who cares?

I've learned one thing: there's a limit to how much crying you can do in a day. The first time I hit this threshold, I got scared. After six hours of reeling through the chaos of grief, suddenly I stopped feeling. I stopped thinking. I stopped crying. There was nothing in my mind or my heart. I was a zombie, going from one room to another with no purpose or task or reason for being there.

What was happening? Was I a cold, heartless mother? Was I like one of those characters on *Law and Order?* The kind of mother who hears the news of her dead child, gives a short cry and then answers all the questions the police need to ask. Was that the kind of person I was?

It becomes even more problematic when I have to talk to people while I'm in this state. While they cry profusely, I hold up my end with objective details of your death, the process of getting your body home, the setting of a date for the funeral. Although I apologize for being in a trance and "cried-out," I hate this absence of pain and feeling. I want to accept this numbness as normal, but when I'm there, it feels like the most abnormal thing a mother can do.

Sleep seems to be the only way to pull out. Every morning I wake up crying again. I cry over you all day long, great sobs of grief every time someone walks through the door. I cry on my own, with my sister, with your buddies, and with Christine and Lenny and Marlene.

Then I go numb and icy again around dinnertime.

And so it goes, day after day after day.

I don't want to shut down, even for a few hours, over you. I want you to see my grief 24/7. I want it to be pure and deep and covered in endless tears of missing you and not wanting you gone.

MOM XXOO

◆   ◆   ◆

Mom,

I wish I could let you know that I feel your grief, whether you are crying, shaking, or walking around in a stupor. These are only different faces of the same thing. I see you moving through a dense cloud of sadness that follows you wherever you go. Sometimes it makes you cry, sometimes it makes you shake and shudder, and sometimes you are only able to exist as an automaton within its grasp.

It's not like I'm watching you, accepting some of your behaviors, rejecting others, and making a tally at the end of each day. Your pain washes over me, but where I am, feelings aren't handled or lived with; just recognized.

I know you love me, and that's all that matters.

Your son, Sam

WHERE ARE YOU?

January

Hi, honey,

Here's something I don't understand—why don't you hover over us like I thought all spirits did for a few days or months after death?

My mother did; I remember it very well. I felt her presence for about four months after she died, although she was not a ghost or anything like that. It was as if she were looking down on me, making sure I was OK. I remember this because I couldn't make love while her spirit was around; that just wasn't something I could do in front of my mother.

With you, though, there's nothing. Sometimes I think you might be watching me as I curl up on the couch, peering at yet another ten o'clock crime drama on TV. I imagine you sneering at my endless appetite for such schlock, but when I explore the notion, I have to admit it's just me wishing for your sneer.

You don't come in dreams, either, as I hoped you would. My sleep is black and empty, with no images, no unfolding stories, no journeys through the past or the chaotic present. I've had a few dreams in which I'm telling someone that you died, and I wake up crying. But it's all me, really. You are nowhere to be found.

Your brother is waiting for you too. During the first few days after you died, Riel would rush off to bed at night for a meeting with you. That was the only time, in fact, when he looked a little cheerful, as if expecting that something positive might happen in an otherwise completely negative world. But you never came to him either, and I stopped asking him about his dreams. I knew the minute he got up, covered in sadness, looking for some coffee, that nothing had transpired during the night.

Part of me thinks your spirit stayed in Africa. I read a book set in Botswana a few months ago, and there they believe that spirits stay where a person dies. This is possible, I think to myself: you were so happy in Ghana, perhaps you stayed. But I still don't understand why, before you settled, you couldn't make a brief appearance for us.

Sometimes I joke with Riel—"I've been trying to tell Sam to go north to Europe and then take a sharp left. Do you think he can find his way back?" I'm just kidding, but each time I say it, I have to remind myself that spirits don't move over land and through air to be with someone … I guess.

Do you remember Elana, my friend with the short black hair, the one who moved to Toronto? Elana had a dream, a couple of days after you died, in which you were standing behind me in my office while I was on the phone, arranging to bring your body back. You were trying to get my attention. But I was so involved in the conversation that I did not see you. Then I started walking down the hall, and you came up behind me, put your arms around my shoulders, and nuzzled me in my neck. But I was oblivious to you in her dream.

You can imagine how I cried when she told me this. There I was, once again, caught up in a task at hand, too busy to see that you had come to me. As we both know, it was my great weakness as a mother: I was often too busy.

You must know, if you're around, how much I want to see you just one more time. Even if you only appear as a feeling, I need so much to say good-bye to you and send just one last piece of love in your direction for you to take with you wherever you have to go. I need one last connection between us to take with me wherever I have to go now.

There's so much about this death thing that I don't understand. Did you come, and I didn't notice? Did you leave completely because there were no loose ends between us? Is there a statute of limitations on showing up as a spirit on earth? Have I missed my chance, or can you still come and wrap your arms around me when I am ready to recognize you? How do I get ready for something like that?

Perhaps I am just trying to change the unchangeable: a person who dies is gone forever from this life. Period. Waiting for dreams and hovering spirits is just a sign that I am not ready to let you go.

If you can't come back for one last good-bye, would you at least give me some idea about what's going on?

Forever, your Mom

◆ ◆ ◆

Mom,

I wish I could help you here, but I can't. For me to come to you, I would have to have some unfinished business with you. But I don't. When I was dying and thought of you, I had no regrets or things unsaid to trouble me. I knew you loved me, and I said good-bye from that hospital bed. I was ready to go.

Grandma was not ready to die. I know that both our deaths dropped from the sky for you, but they were really quite different. I had time to close my relationships in my heart. Your mother went so quickly in that car crash that I imagine she had to do her "settling" after the fact. I suspect that's why she stuck around for a while.

The truth of the matter is that it is not you, the living, who determine a spirit's time on earth. I would like to comfort you or offer you that one last chance to say "Good-bye," but that's not the deal.

Eventually you will see that my absence is the greatest gift you could have given me. The love between us was solid and sent me on my way. My life was short but finished. Though I might have accomplished more, I was content with what I did in twenty-five years.

Perhaps, when you finally let me go, I can meet you in a dream. Not to say "Good bye," but "Hello" again.

I love you.

Sam

RELIEF

January

Dear Sam,

Confession: I worried about you all the time. I kept it to myself because I knew you needed to feel support, not anxiety. But I fretted all the time. I worried when you moved to Ottawa to live alone and prove your independence. I agonized when you worked so hard on your business proposal and then couldn't find a partner. I was scared that people would take advantage of you in Africa. I worried about what you would do when you came back here.

Shortly after you died, I actually felt some relief that you would not have to return to Montreal. I had this vision of you arriving back and once again feeling the pressure to go back to school, with the odds in favor of failure no matter how much support we found for you. I could see your frustration while looking for jobs that didn't require French, thinking about moving away but not wanting to go, trying to get friends back after such a long absence.

Finally, I thought, hard times are over for you.

I felt shameful, almost dirty, the first time I had this thought. I tried to hide it the minute it first emerged. I pushed it away as quickly as I could, hoping it would never return. It comes perilously close to feeling relief that you died. I bury it deeper each time it appears, but it won't go away and keeps coming back in all its ugliness.

To make matters worse, I'm sure you know when I'm thinking this. I imagine you hearing my thoughts, feeling betrayed that your main supporter has turned evil protector after your death.

Please believe me: I don't want you gone just because life was some-times difficult for you. It's just that I have always felt your pain and frus-trations even when I was cheering you on from battle to battle.

But I guess I can't keep all my demons backstage. If it comes up again and you see it, I am so sorry, Sam.

Your far-from-perfect Mother

◆   ◆   ◆

Mom,

Yes, I was surprised the first time those thoughts appeared. If I had been alive, I would have been very hurt and disappointed. I would have wondered if you blamed me for getting sick and screwing everything up for myself and everyone else.

But the crazy thing about this dying business is that I see things more clearly. When I was alive, you acted as my champion, not my protector. Some-times I had a glimpse that you were worried, but it was always overshadowed by your encouragement to move forward and take on the next dream. I never doubted your support, and I don't doubt it now.

Glad that I died? Don't be ridiculous. That would mean that all your sor-row is fake. You're not that good an actress.

Relief that there will be no more pain for me? I feel that too. Since you were the main person helping me through each depressing failure and frustration, those moments probably loomed larger for you. Go ahead and feel the relief. Life is not all roses and candy, and there's nothing wrong with being glad that some of the bad times are over.

But they were only a small part of my life. You were pivotal in leading me out of those dark periods and into my accomplishments. That's what I hope you'll remember.

Sam

MY PREMONITION

January

After Midnight ...

A dream: I'm sitting across from the astrologer I saw last summer (a birthday present from Shirley). The astrologer's predictions tumble onto the table, and I am reminded of what she says to me: "The conflicts of the last seven years are over, and you are entering the best time of your life. You will travel the world with your work. You will have money again, and new relationships will inspire you. You will not die from a lingering illness but will be taken quickly, while away from home. You will die suddenly in Africa or Egypt, and your body will be shipped home in a box."

I awaken with a terrible jolt. She was talking about Sam! I am outraged. How could she make such a mistake? Or did she know it was Sam and try to protect me? If she had said something, I could have steered him to India or Latin America for his trip. I want to blame his death on her, but that's crazy, irrational. Still, the anger stays, boiling, with no place to go.

Were there other signs that I didn't notice?

◆　　◆　　◆

Dear Sam,

For five days after you left for Africa, I couldn't sleep. As you know, this is completely out of character. I fall asleep immediately and stay dead to the world through anything: you or Riel coming in too late; a booming, all-night party upstairs; thunderstorms that wake the whole city except for me.

But once you left on your trip, I tossed and turned all night. It was not typical insomnia in which the body lies inert and exhausted while the mind races through a kaleidoscope of dizzying images from one's waking life. This was different: a physical ache, with no images appearing behind my closed eyes.

It was a hollow feeling, black and deep, like a misplaced muscle cramp that had roamed from the legs into the pelvis and back again. Other times, it felt as if sharp rocks had lodged themselves in the pit of my stomach. It made no sense. You'd been away from home before on trips to the States, travel with Katimavik, and excursions like tree planting, and I never had trouble sleeping or felt sick to my stomach.

When it was happening, I figured it was because I couldn't imagine Africa ... or you there. I had no pictures in my head of that country, no idea of where you were, no concept of how hot it was, and no certainty about whether you could understand the language or find your way through town. I couldn't picture a house, your room or your walk to work every day; even a spurious image, an inaccurate fantasy did not show itself to me. You had just gone off, and until I heard from you, there was a black space in my head with your name on it.

The minute I got your first e-mails from Africa, those feelings left, and I started sleeping soundly again. So I tidied up the experience into a neat package, labeled it "What happens when you can't imagine something," and filed it away.

A couple of days after you died, when I was in the first throes of mourning, I remembered these feelings because I was having them again. My stomach felt like it had shards of glass in it. That same ache in my pelvis was back.

I almost vomited when I made the connection: I had known you were going to die. I had felt the pain of your death months ago.

From that moment of realization, the "what ifs" and "shoulds" began haunting me. I fantasized dozens of scenarios that might have saved your life.

In an e-mail to you in London, I could have written: "Come back, Sam. NOW! I think you're going to die in Africa." But then I imagined your reply: "Mom, don't go nuts on me. Everyone is great. I feel fantastic. I thought you supported me in this trip."

I could have called you in Africa more often, making sure you were taking your malaria medication, doing more research on possible health calamities that might hit you, grilling you on how you were holding up physically in the new climate. But, then again, your probable response to my nervous inquiries would have been, "Ma, I'm taking my medicine. Why are you on my case? I've been taking seizure pills for years and never missing them once. Why don't you think I'm doing it now? I really don't need to hear this. It sounds like you don't think I can handle my own life." And my ridiculous rebuttal: "I do. I do. But I just have this feeling you're going to die."

I try to exonerate myself with the realization that I didn't know that I was scared for your life. And even if I'd known, none of my imagined attempts to save you would have brought you home.

That being said, I still feel guilty: a part of me knew this was going to happen, and perhaps there was something I could have done to change everything.

Mom XXOO

◆   ◆   ◆

Mom,

I was relieved to hear about your premonition of my death. You know, I had a similar feeling myself, and my premonition also went unrecognized until it was too late to turn around.

I was at the airport with Lenny and Marlene and getting my bags out of the trunk. I said my usual good-byes, hugged and kissed them both, then made my way to the entrance doors. Just as I was walking in, something made me turn around. Without thinking, I walked back and hugged Dad one more time, this time deeper and closer than before. Afterwards, while I stood in line for my ticket, I thought about what had happened. I decided I hugged him again to soothe his worries about my trip.

I see now that I must have known it was the last time I would ever see him and wanted him to know how very much I love him. Like you, I wonder if I could have walked away from my trip, knowing this might be my last good-bye to you both. Probably not.

Your loving son, Sam

NO LOOSE ENDS—YOUR FATE?

February

My dear Sam,

Have you noticed how neat and tidy everything was at your death? You may have been only twenty-five and cut down earlier than most, but your life seems not to have ended in the middle of a chapter but at a solid conclusion of *Part III: Young Adulthood.*

This realization was one of those insights that came flying out of nowhere the other day. I balked at its appearance, but when I quickly listed your goals and dreams, I found them accomplished.

Your seizures always tested your independence, and going off to Africa (not to mention handling your death alone) showed that you definitely had learned to take charge of your own life.

You realized that working with children was your calling and had the courage to pursue it without a degree, outside of a box that, in our society, would have kept you at the bottom of a career ladder. From what the people at the day care in Africa wrote to us, your talent with the kids there was recognized in a different way than on this side of the world. I'm so thankful that you had the chance to feel admiration and respect from others. You deserved it.

You fell in love just before leaving and experienced the thrill of having someone devoted to you, loving you, and sharing a closeness that only comes with an intimate relationship.

It always bothered you that Riel and I were writers, while you had difficulty putting even the simplest of sentences together. Yet your e-mails from Africa are a wonderful legacy from a blossoming writer. It was so exciting for me to watch your writing skills catch up with your thoughts and observations. Your last e-mails describing your trip to the north during the Christmas holidays were particularly rich with details and discoveries.

Although you never had children of your own, the kids at Kamp Kanawana and in the Kumasi day care all called you "Daddy" and relied on you to care for and nurture them. You parented.

I don't know if you were aware of these accomplishments, but I like to think they made it easier for you to accept your death and that when you were dying, there was a feeling of completion about your life.

For me, it's different. It's like a surprise ending in a movie: after the film is complete, you realize that all the plot points were resolved without your being aware of it. While I admire the skill it took to bring it all together, a part of me feels stupid for not seeing the overall picture before now.

More importantly, though, I don't want it to make sense. I want the neatness of it all to be horrific, not a solid argument that there's such a thing as fate.

I keep wondering why I thought going off to Africa was a beginning for you when, in hindsight, it all pointed to an ending.

Your hopelessly blinded Mother

◆   ◆   ◆

Mom,

This is definitely one of your glass-half-empty moments. Why are you not comforted by the fullness of my life? Others who lose children have to mourn lives barely begun or cut short before any lessons are learned or any feats accomplished. In many ways, I was fortunate to have lived as long as I did.

I wasn't really conscious of what I had resolved or accomplished before I died. But there was a sense of peace that enveloped me when I was sick, and that might have been this neat-ending feeling you are talking about.

I don't regret that I was too busy experiencing my life to foresee where it was headed. Isn't that what living in the present is all about? Isn't that what we're supposed to do—embrace each moment and live it to the fullest?

I know you miss me, but somewhere down the road, you will have to accept my death. And when you do, please be happy for me and for what I managed to pack in during my twenty-five years on earth.

Sammy

THE SAD CELEBRITY

February

Sam the Man,

Here's a bizarre twist: your death has turned me into a well-known tragic figure in the community. I have achieved some macabre celebrity status. People are watching my every move, talking about me, asking one another how I can possibly cope with this situation. Sometimes people tell me about these conversations, but I am too battered to care what they think. I want to hear their observations in case they have some insights, but I am too caught up in the unsolicited sorrow that fills my days and nights.

I watch each person I meet checking my "state" against his or her recent conclusions about how I'm coping. Don't get me wrong: this is the most gentle, caring attention I've ever received, albeit continuous and intrusive. From George and Costas at PA Supermarché to the insufferable Philippe, the pharmacist, from our landlord to Pascale at the restaurant down the street, the concern is of an intensity normally reserved for only the dearest of friends.

The fact is that your death and my handling of it touch every person who hears about it, regardless of education, wealth, gender, or culture. It's one of those universal nightmares that everyone knows could happen to them.

But it makes me feel ill at ease to be the center of attention because of your death. As both of us know, you are not the first kid to die, and I am not the first mother to lose a son. When you think about it, all over the world, mothers are losing their sons, and young husbands are dying in war. Most of the survivors have to brush themselves off and get immediately back to the task of surviving. They have no time to weep for weeks, write down their emotions, consider and discuss the fine points of mourning.

Even in our culture, what I am going through is not as unique as it feels. Every day we are reminded of tragedy: teenagers crash into trees after parties, planes fall from the sky, thousands die during political hostilities they barely understand, and babies don't wake up from SIDS. Some parents lose more than one child; sometimes whole families are wiped out. It's the nature of life that not all of us make it into old age.

In the grander scheme of things, we don't deserve celebrity status. We are merely a close-to-home example of the fact that life is fragile and can end at any time—poof!

Then again, if it happened to someone else, I would be among others watching, imagining and commenting on how that person was coping.

Your Mom

WHY DIDN'T YOU TELL US YOU WERE SICK?

March

Dear Sam,

I have gone over and over the fact that you would not let Tina and Koffi call us when you went into the hospital. I have tried to see if from your point of view, but I am stuck with wanting it to have happened differently. A useless hope, I know, but something I can't shake.

I see you leaving the house with Koffi on your way to the hospital. So sick you cannot walk without help, your legs always giving out because of seizure tremors you are too weak to control.

I see you in the hospital bed, the doctors and nurses taking your blood, telling you that malaria has set in but that you will be better in a few days. When Koffi arrives to see how you are doing, he pleads with you to call your parents. But you tell him, "No. I will call them when I am better in a couple of days. No need for them to worry."

I know our reactions would have upset you. Lenny would have been sick with fear, thinking that such an outcome was exactly why he did not want you to go so far away by yourself. I would have gone straight into panic mode, phoning the doctors, trying to get more information and making a general nuisance of myself. Yes, I would also have arranged to get on a plane as soon as possible in order to be there with you and make sure you got good care.

And then I realize that was exactly why you didn't call. In true Sammy style, you wanted to handle this challenge by yourself. You wanted to get better and then call us to report that all was now well and you were back at work.

Good plan, except things didn't turn out that way. I know you didn't figure out, until it was too late, just how sick you were. And I can't be angry at you for not knowing.

But your insistence on handling this by yourself robbed us of being with you at the end.

If we had known you were sick, we could have at least had a couple of last words with you. I have imagined that phone call over and over in my head: "Sammy, are they taking good care of you? You'll get better, and I'm coming down in the next few days. We love you so much. Just take it easy. I'll be there soon." It would have been something for you to look forward to. Even though you would have died before I got there, I could have been part of your final days. The news of your death would not have come from the detectives at the door, but from people who loved you and gave you a home in Africa. I would have been able to be with your body on the trip home. I could have…. I would have …

I know these could-have-been scenarios bring only futile feelings that tear me apart rather than help me heal. Wishes, just out of reach, that lead nowhere. Wanting you to have acted out of character, not as the twenty-five-year-old kid that you were. But part of me holds onto the notion that, if we had known you were sick, the shock of your death would have been less traumatic.

It's a lot to expect from a simple phone call, but I dream of a last sound of your voice to carry with me in my heart.

MOM XXOO

◆   ◆   ◆

Mom,

I know. I know. But it's not easy on this end either, realizing I made a crucial mistake at the end. I have to accept that, as you said, I was a kid who didn't know any better. All my energy was focused first on trying to get better and then on leaving your world peacefully.

Even if we'd had a phone call or two, my death would have been a tremendous shock. You would have never believed, either at home or on a plane ride over, that I would actually die. However, I can see now that some last words would have given you a kind of closure that you don't have with the way things actually worked out. And I am sorry for taking that away from you.

But with all our mistakes in life, is that one really so important in the long run? You know I loved you all. You know I was thinking of you as I was dying.

And I know you can still hear my voice in your heart—from better, happier times.

Sam

DEATH BECOMES YOU

March

Dear Sam,

I sensed early on that to accept your death, I would have to accept your life as a twenty-five-year entity. Not as fifty years cut in half. Not as twenty-five years of experience and many more years of unfulfilled dreams. Just twenty-five years from beginning to end. That's what I have to acknowledge and live with.

What surprises me is how the story of your life changed so dramatically when "sudden death" was tacked onto the end.

Forget the sense of struggle and plodding through life that you often felt about your adventures. When the final tally was in, it turns out you were going at breakneck speed.

Suddenly we see someone who traveled all over Canada and the States, then Africa, making you the envy of your brother (yes, it's true) and a brave man to your friends. In your unrelenting quest for meaningful work, you cuddled abused aboriginal kids in Saskatchewan, built an Olympic luge run in Barrie, Ontario, and fished for lobster in Tatamacouche, Nova Scotia, while you were with Katimavik. In your two and a half months in Africa, you traveled over three-quarters of Ghana and left an entire village mourning your death.

Without learning how to spell, you sent inspired e-mails from Ghana. You had a first love, won the top award at Kamp, and handled your seizures with such grace that many of your friends at the memorial service were surprised to learn that you still had them.

I'm sure you didn't plan it, but you did manage a most dramatic exit. And such a powerful, final signature casts a different perspective on the years lived.

I was always proud of you, but now I admire you. I really do. I hope you know.

Love, Mom

◆　　◆　　◆

Mom, you're right: it's a strange thing how death changes life. While living, I went from one plan to another, only feeling a blank, fuzzy future and never noticing what was building up from the past. It was only when my life was finished that I saw the whole picture. And wow, even I was surprised.

I wish I could have seen it before. It would have made me feel better about myself and more confident that my life was full even without a clear path to follow.

I don't suppose you can learn from this for yourself?

Sam

TALKING TO YOU

March

Dear Sam,

Yesterday, I realized I've started talking to you in my head. The topic on the table at the time was philosophic: "Will I be a better person once I accept your death?" When I think about these big-picture concepts now, I look to you for an answer.

The fact is that if you were still alive and that question came out of my mouth, you would roll your eyes and leave the room. At twenty-five, who gives a shit?

Did you grow up before you died, or have I just changed my image of you?

Love, Mom

◆　　　◆　　　◆

This is an easy one, Mom. Those big picture questions and concepts rarely entered my life before I died. I do remember thinking a bit about death when Drew died and also when all those kids from my high school were killed in that car crash. But I never came up with any ideas because I still had no sense of actually living … or dying, for that matter. That's why rolling my eyes would have been exactly my response to you.

Times have changed now. It's not that I've grown up … it's that these are the only topics that matter.

But I still have to roll my eyes at you thinking you'd get an answer out of me.

Sam

FINDING A PLACE FOR YOU IN THE HOUSE

March

Samboni,

Remember how I convinced you to pack up your things and store them in containers before you left for Africa to keep them safe and ready for your return? At first you balked at the idea—this was just another one of my attempts to organize you. Then you remembered that while you were gone, Riel would probably find and adopt your hooded sweatshirts, and I might sneak a sweater or two of yours that I liked. So, to keep your stuff safe from our itchy fingers, you crammed it all in a couple of big plastic containers and put them on the top shelf of the pantry.

So here we are: you're not coming back, and all signs of you are packed neatly away. While I can't bring myself to take down those containers, I don't want reminders of you stored away in a dark closet either. Yes, there are photos of you here and there, but that's not special enough. I want a permanent place for you on Park Avenue.

When I mentioned this idea to a couple of friends, they referred to it as making a shrine. I was horrified at the notion: every fiber in me rejected the idea of you as some kind of son-saint on an altar. I just wanted a corner that I could pass in the course of a day and be flooded with memories of you.

I decided to tackle this project on your birthday, and it certainly beat weeping around the house, a very un-birthday type of behavior.

I finally settled on the cabinet that your dad and I found one summer in an alley. It now stands in the entrance, storing hats and gloves inside, its top surface used only for the odd piece of junk mail that doesn't make it to the recycle bin right away.

I gathered some of your treasures, as well as some items that remind me of you. I brought out a small wooden box that your Grandma Lorna once gave me because it resembles the lovely carved coffin they sent you home in. I filled it with the Ghanaian money that I found in your wallet and the engraved silver bracelet that you received on your thirteenth birthday, the one that I tried to wear but was scared I would lose. Next to the box, I put the elephant candle holder that you and Riel bought for me one Christmas and a word-search puzzle from the book we kept in the bathroom (with your signature scrawled across the bottom of the page, something you always added when you completed one).

On the wall behind the cabinet, I hung several pictures of you: the two of us from the Christmas before you left (I love your smile in that picture); you at about age three with your lovely red hair and Superman T-shirt; and two of the pictures you took in Africa. One shows the elephant you saw up north, and in the other one, you are posing with a child from the day care. Both of you are grinning, proud to be holding each other's hand.

Whenever I walk in the door, you are the first thing I see. It's not the same as hearing "Mom, is that you?" from the living room couch, but it's a greeting and a reminder that you are still in my life.

Love ya, Sam.

◆   ◆   ◆

Mom,

I'm very touched by the place you've created for me. You don't have to worry about it being a shrine. It's nothing like that. When you think about it, it's kinda like what you gave me in the past: a place in your house if I ever needed it.

I don't need to be there so much now as I want to be there. And you found a way to bring me inside. Thanks, Mom.

Sam

HEAVEN IN SEVEN

April

Dear Super-Sam,

The Habs made it to the quarter-finals last night, pulling themselves up from a 1-3 position down to the Boston Bruins. People were dancing in the streets; Parc Lafontaine was mobbed with screaming fans. I'm hoping you were watching from a ringside seat in the cosmic "reds."

It's been two or three weeks since I cried, but today, the morning after this magic victory, I can't seem to stop. In the middle of writing an e-mail, I get a flash of you: the instant a goal is scored, you spring off the orange chair in front of the TV, demanding high fives all around. I jump every time the phone rings, thinking it's you calling to berate me for having dinner with Melanie instead of watching the game. I want to come home and see you at the dining room table, reading every sports section you can find to prolong the joy.

Each mental image brings on the tears, and I wonder how I'm going to get through the quarter-finals with Tampa Bay.

While writing this, I realized I don't even know the score of the game. I go to the *Gazette* and stop dead in my tracks at the front-page headline: IT'S HEAVEN IN SEVEN.

You wrote that, didn't you?

Mom

◆   ◆   ◆

Mom,

I can't believe you didn't watch the game. Dinner with Melanie is such a regular affair. This was history, and you missed it. Hopefully, Riel gave you shit about it since I wasn't there. I do miss my Habs.

Sam

THE MISTAKE FANTASY

April

Sammy,

The other day the doorbell rang, and the first thought that came into my head was that it was someone from the Department of Foreign Affairs. They were coming to tell me there had been a huge mistake, that you had been traveling—you were not dead—and you would call me in the next few days.

This is not the first time I have imagined this. But it's curious that after so many months, I still cling to it. Once it arrives, this fantasy doesn't disappear easily. I have such an intense desire for it to be true that it lingers even through the next, persistent knock.

The only way I have found to shut this fantasy out is to force myself to bring up the vision of your corpse. I need absolute proof to dispel this hope. The image of your cold body is the only antidote that works.

When I decided to see your corpse many months ago, I said to myself that it was important to face reality. I thought I only needed to see it once, so that I could move on and really grieve.

It turns out that I have to face your body over and over again. The ring of the phone, the doorbell, those pictures in the hallway that bring you back to life, a stray sock in a drawer that's waiting for your foot, your handwriting in a cookbook you once gave me for Christmas: they all take me to a place where some official comes to apologize for getting you mixed up with someone else or losing track of you in Africa while you traveled.

I have never wanted a dream to come true as much as I want the Mistake Fantasy. And I have never had such solid proof in my head that it can't happen.

I guess I still have a long way to go.

Mom

75

◆   ◆   ◆

Mom,

I think you are farther along than you give yourself credit for. At the beginning, you were going through all those "what ifs" to prevent the thing from happening in the first place. Now you've got the death and the corpse squarely in front of you. You're just wishing it would all go away.

Can't blame you for that.

Sam

SEEING YOU ON THE STREET

April

Dear Sam,

The other day, I was walking to pick up Melanie's car. Crossing the street toward the Delphi Variety Store, out of the corner of my eye, I saw you walking down Fairmont Street. There was that slight awkwardness in your step. You had your backpack hanging off one shoulder and, though your face was turned away toward a store window, I knew it was you.

My legs immediately buckled, and I grabbed onto a nearby stop sign to keep from falling down. My stomach somersaulted, and I wanted to cry and vomit at the same time.

When I looked again, the guy was closer and did not resemble you at all. But reality was not enough to stop my heart from pounding or put my stomach back in its place.

I pulled myself together and continued walking, but the event changed my world once again. The dreamy, surreal quality of my life, which had just begun to fade, came back with a vengeance. I walked on as a woman who couldn't trust herself to see what was really there.

What most worries me about this experience is whether I will start seeing you all over the place: in every little red-haired kid who skips down the street, every handsome teenager stepping onto a bus, every story of a child with seizures, or any young person planning a trip to Africa. Will thousands of everyday occurrences start bringing me to my knees?

Or maybe you were making an appearance through that guy on the street, and I should have shown a little openness to the ways of the spirit. If

I really believed you might show yourself that way, shouldn't it soothe me rather than throwing me into turmoil?

I feel so unequipped to handle all this. I keeping wanting you to come into my world in some way, and then when I see someone who looks like you, I collapse. Is there any way to tell the difference between a real visit of the spirit and a figment of my imagination?

Your very confused Mother

◆   ◆   ◆

Dear Mom,

First of all, I did not inhabit that guy walking down Fairmont. If I were going to inhabit someone, it would be a good lookin' girl! But he did have a few of my characteristics, so it's not hard to understand your reaction.

Right now, everything and everyone resembling me or any part of my life is going to take you straight to the realization that I'm dead. It's this fact you're trying to come to terms with. I guess your heart is making sure you don't lose sight of reality, no matter how painful it still is.

The good news, however, is that once you accept my death, all these little connections to me will become reminders of wonderful times together. A walk down Fairmont Street will take you past the place where I was born. Delphi Variety will remind you how we both looked forward to getting stamps from the feisty ladies behind the counter.

And that's just for starters.

Sam

HARDEST THING IN THE WORLD

April

Sammy,

I'm having a lot of trouble responding to people's reactions to your death. It's nothing to do with their concern or motivations. Everyone is genuinely upset, and you can see the care with which they approach me. But each encounter throws me off balance, and I'm never sure what to do.

Most often, people ask me how I'm doing. What is normally a routine greeting has become a sincere query about my state of mind. I can't say "Fine" because that would be a blatant lie. "Coping" is a typically pat answer, but I feel that it tells them nothing about how a person actually survives such an ordeal … and I can see in their eyes that they want a bit of truth in return.

It's so hard to know what or how much to say. Each person is different. Some would be quite happy for me to spill my heart out. Others are concerned but reluctant to go very deep into the matter. On certain days, I have to match the response to the person several dozen times. I am exhausted by it all, something I never expected.

There's one observation I keep hearing that troubles me: "It's so unnatural for a parent to lose a child." I probably would say the same thing to anyone else in this situation. But now that I'm here, I can't see that it would feel any better or any more natural to lose a spouse, a parent, or a close friend.

Maybe I'm different from other parents. I never had conscious daydreams, now shattered, of Christmas twenty years from now, with me as a grandmother and both you and Riel arriving for dinner with your wives and children. Not that I thought it wouldn't happen, but I gave up predicting the future a long time ago. But it does seem strange (unnatural?) to imagine twenty more Christmases without you, your wife, and your children.

When people say that dealing with a child's death is the hardest thing in the world, I have to agree that I have never faced anything else so horrific in my own life. But why diminish the impact of deaths that are not the deaths of children? I've been to two funerals since your death, and each time my condolences have been answered with: "Well, it's nothing like what you went through." I don't want special treatment while others are mourning. I want them to come up to me and say they are losing their minds and ask me what to do. Not that I could say, but I want my loss to draw me closer to others, not set me apart.

As time goes on, I find myself being more and more of a hermit. I stay home most evenings, only going out to convince myself I have not become a shut-in. It's not that I don't want to see people. It's that I can't bear to hear over and over again how unnatural and hard this whole thing is.

Tell me something I don't know.

Mom

◆   ◆   ◆

Ramblings ...

Sometimes I think what people are really saying is that I should have died instead of Sam. It doesn't feel like my time to die, but perhaps I should be wishing it otherwise. To make myself feel better, I imagine Sam and myself in front of a firing squad, and the executioner says that one of us must die. I know I would offer myself up without hesitation, and it would be the parent in me stepping forward. But I would not be acting to keep the natural order of things. I would make that choice because I love Sam so much and would want to give him more time if I could.

◆   ◆   ◆

Mom,

Having trouble responding to people's concern must be a shock for you, Den Mother to the world.

I doubt that others expect you to always have the perfect response. Just as they stumble through their condolences, you can stumble through your responses. As long as you respect the feelings of others, you can pretty much say whatever you want, and people will understand.

From where I am, I see the people around you trying very hard to give you the space you need to grieve. When they say it's the hardest thing in the world, they are really saying, "We can't imagine what you have to do, so take as long as you need."

It really is unnatural for a child to die before his parents. It goes against the cycle of life. There's no specific feeling attached to this truth. It just is. And you're right: it explains why my death has rocked you so deeply, while your mother's death, though very upsetting, did not cause the same kind of upheaval in your life.

Still, all this has nothing to do with your death. That will come when it comes, in your own time. Not one person thinks you should take my place, although each would understand the comfort of your firing squad fantasy.

You might want to open up a bit to what others are trying to say to you. Feel the love in their words, not the challenge. That might get you out of the house and back into the fold.

Sam

MOTHER'S DAY

May

Sammy,

It's almost Mother's Day, and I've been very weepy as it approaches. I was talking to your dad, and in the middle of our conversation, I just started bawling: "I don't want to have Mother's Day without Sam."

On the day itself, I was out in the country with Josh and Ingrid when their son, Daniel, came in with flowers for both Ingrid and me for Mother's Day. As his little hands thrust the roses at me, I was overcome with sadness and tears. I couldn't even say "Thank You."

I can see so clearly my little redheaded kid trotting behind his big brother Riel as he carried the tray with burnt toast, orange juice, and a rose stuck in a plastic glass, wobbling in the center of the tray. While your brother played the part of "cool dude" with the breakfast, you simply stood over my bed and beamed with accomplishment.

Riel will carry on our tradition this year by himself: breakfast and flowers. But I will be waiting for you to walk in the door with one lily for me, as you did last year.

I will always be

Your Mother

◆　　◆　　◆

Ramblings ...

Thank God I had two children. Having Riel still around allows me to stay a mother, and I am so grateful for that.

But I see that Riel feels, as I do, that we have become a kind of broken family. Not dysfunctional, but incomplete. We cling to each other in a way we never did before. Sometimes we seem more like a couple than a family unit. It's not discussed, but even the everyday hugs have more intensity than before ... as if we want to leave some closeness behind each time.

I have been having fantasies of adopting a child. I imagine a nine- or ten-year-old girl moving into the house and myself juggling work and her demands. I want to feel the constraints of raising a kid. I want there to be not enough time to do everything. Although Riel has another brother and sister from Lenny and Marlene, I want to give him another sibling from my side.

But I don't think I will do it. It's only me wanting to go back to a time when mothering was my main occupation, when two kids were always competing for my time, when confusion and chaos prevailed, and when my dreams for my kids were still infinite.

YOUR PRESENCE IN THE COUNTRY

June

Samboni,

Deep waves of missing you slide over me as I look out over the hills in Knowlton from the house I am renting again this summer. Unlike other triggers that bring on these feelings, it's not because I remember times with you here. You never visited my country place ... there was always too much to do in the city.

But you are here, and I can feel your spirit in the trees, the wind, the sound of the birds. This person out here isn't Sam, my child, but what you have become now that your life is over. A part of the life cycle in which spirits come to earth as humans and then go back into something bigger, some place that hovers just on the edge of all nature.

You probably think this is crazy, knowing the truth about these matters from your vantage point. But this view at least explains to me why you seem so near in the fields of Town Hall Road and so absent on Park Avenue in the city.

There's so much I don't understand about the after-death realm and the spirit world. Sometimes I envy people who have solid beliefs about these things or have a religion that lays out the answers that they accept and hold onto.

But I have neither. I'm just a single human being trying to piece together my feelings into some fabric that contains both heart and soul. Your death has taught me there's a difference: my soul feels your presence, my heart feels your absence.

Out here in the country, my heart and soul seemed joined together. As I sit on the porch, the soft breeze in the trees covers me with memories of you. At first they are warm and wonderful images: your smile when you request something "light" for dinner with no idea what that means; you looking in the mirror at the buzz-cut I just gave you, always finding fault with your sideburns; you giving me a sleepy morning hello and a hug. I understand, for a fleeting moment, what others mean when they tell me that eventually, when I think of you, I will remember all the good times and the love we shared.

Then another breeze blows over me, and I run from the porch, barely making it to the bushes out of everyone's earshot. My legs give out; on my hands and knees, I give in to spasms of wailing, grief turned to nausea, a heart that feels like it's breaking into a thousand pieces of jagged glass.

And I can't see how any notion, however lofty, will ever take this pain away.

MOM XXOO

◆　　　◆　　　◆

It is so hard for me to see you struggle like this. Especially since I cannot help you at all.

What you and others believe is neither right nor wrong. People create their beliefs to explain the unexplainable to themselves. That is the purpose they serve during life. Once you die, the whole game changes, and this is not something you can know until you are there.

I don't know what to tell you. Perhaps you need some beliefs about spirituality. Perhaps you just need a lot more time to heal.

I'm sorry I can't take your hand and bring you to the peace you need. All I can do is assure you that you are strong enough and smart enough to figure it out.

Sam

PRODUCING THE PERFECT MOURNING SHOW

July

Dear Sam,

I know you will find this typical of me, but I feel as if I'm really screwing up this mourning business. I so wanted to go through it with grace and purpose. I wanted to bring just the right amounts of strength and vulnerability to the experience. I didn't want to lose my grip, but neither did I want to try to control the damn thing. I wanted you to be proud that I was grieving in the proper way.

Proper? Any grief counselor worth his or her salt would dismiss the word immediately. I can hear what that counselor would say without even making an appointment: "Each person has their own time and particular journey to follow. There's no proper route."

But it's so complicated. I feel as if I'm on some sort of bizarre train trip, one in which the train moves only if I complete certain tasks, and there's no conductor to tell me what these tasks are or when they are complete. Am I crying enough, repressing too much, feeling the right amount of sorrow, moving too fast—or too slowly—through my new life without you? Surely these are the questions. But what are the answers?

I don't think my measure of mourning has to do with what other people think of me. When I encounter someone who knows about your death, I can now talk without feeling the need to look sad or bring tears into the conversation. However, I always mention it in some way: it is, after all, still the most important thing in my life. I don't want anyone to think that I grieved for a few months, and then my life went back to normal.

But if life doesn't go back to normal, how should it change? I think that if I knew the answer to that question, I would know where this train was going, and my tasks would become clear. Is your death a message about living in the moment? Should I reevaluate my work life and start making more time for projects that will make a difference in the world? Do I need to be more careful about my health and stop acting as if I will live forever? Maybe there are people in my life with whom I need to spend more time. What about finally slowing down my pace and making more deliberate decisions about how I spend my time?

The truth is, though, that most of these things are on a list I've been carrying around in my pocket for years, tackling one or two whenever my life seemed to need a push forward. They're good ideas, but they are part of my life, not yours.

But I want to draw a clear line to divide the time *before* and *after* your death. I think of going to Africa to work with AIDS victims and dedicating the rest of my life to helping others. But I can't leave Riel and Lenny right now. I think of selling everything I own, leaving my apartment, and getting a smaller place, filled with just the few things I need to live a simpler life. But I love having guests, and I'm not ready to throw away my past. I think of joining the circus, changing careers, making all new friends.

Surely mourning is not just an experience in and of itself. How can something this intense not leave a mark and force a person to change? But I just don't know where it's pointing and what I'm supposed to do.

I guess I'd better stick to producing television programs for the moment. At least I know what they're about.

Mom

◆　　　◆　　　◆

Ramblings ...

I hate my life right now. I have no enthusiasm for much in it. Work seems superficial and meaningless—who cares if this or that documentary gets made? Whose life will be changed by seeing it? I feel a little better about organizing the benefit for my friend with breast cancer and getting involved with housing for seniors. But I can't make a living off volunteer work. I go out with friends but hear the same conversations over and over again. Are we getting closer or just bumping up against each other so we don't feel completely alone?

Everything has a hollow feel. I want to make big changes but come up with little that excites me. When I do think of something, my motivation disappears. I can't even make a decent To Do List anymore.

A life with no purpose is one thing. A life with no dreams is worse.

◆   ◆   ◆

Dear Mom,

If you don't mind my saying so, you're expecting too much from yourself right now. Yes, mourning is a very intense experience, but it cannot be managed or produced in the way you are trying to do. It's a period in your life when feelings emerge, disappear, and resurface to a rhythm that may not make much sense to you. Using your train metaphor, you are not the conductor or the engineer at the wheel. You are the passenger, responding to what you see from the window and what walks down the aisle to sit next to you.

Your life is changing. I have no doubt about that. But the transformation may not be as visible or physical as you are trying to imagine. It might be something no one else sees, like a deeper layer of your being where death, spirituality, and your life's purpose become companions to whatever you decide to do.

I have only respect for the quality of your grieving. You are not running away from it. You are asking the tough questions. You are feeling what's there.

I'm willing to make a bet with you that your next chapter will be quite different from the life you are leading now. But we would both be crazy to try to predict a date.

Just keep on rolling, and don't deny yourself the euphoria of discovering the surprise at the end of the tracks.

Sam

FAMILY AFFAIRS

August

Sam,

I went out to California for your Aunt Cookie's marriage to Damian. All my sisters and your Grandpa and Carol were there. This is the third time this year that we've gathered from all parts of North America for an occasion. This is the first time it's been for something good.

Being with my five sisters brings your tragedy closer. The absence is always there, but the sense of tragedy comes and goes. Your name comes up often—"Sammy would have loved these cupcakes." "It was weird not putting in Sammy's name for the Christmas draw." "Sometimes I can just hear his voice." We're a family of chatterboxes, so nothing's left unnoticed or unsaid.

The sisters were in charge of getting Cookie and Damian's house ready for the celebration. Since they had just moved in, none of their family photos were on the walls, so I offered to go through their pictures and get them into frames for hanging. While rooting through the picture box, I came across your graduation picture—you know the one: your expression, with that give-away smile, says "Yippee! I made it!" The same photo that several family members refused to accept because it did not reflect of the seriousness of the occasion.

Staring at your picture, I got hit with a wave of pain and longing, something that has diminished over the months but evidently can come back with the ferocity of "news first heard." I'm always glad to be alone when this happens. There's nothing anyone can do, and I feel free to just let it all come out: tears, slobber, runny nose, and all.

Each sister, in her own way, checked in to see how I was doing. I gave them my prepared but honest answer: "I'm healing, but it all comes back regularly, and I wonder if I will ever feel better." In turn, I asked each of them how she thought I was managing. Only Claudia's answer stunned me: "You're the same person, but your spark isn't always there."

Sometimes I fool myself into believing that I appear exactly the same to others as I did before you died. Since I do most of my crying and carrying on by myself, I'm like the kid who closes his eyes and thinks no one can see him.

We are fragile as a family. Losing you and Aunt Allu (one young and one nearly-old) so close together reminds me that families are a center of the life-death cycle—members dying, new ones being born. I'm sure you agree, though, that if your cousins and brother don't get cracking, the deaths are going to hold their lead over the births.

You would have loved Cookie's wedding. We did more than the usual amount of welling up during the ceremony—any life ritual makes the Torge girls weep, as you know—but we balanced that weeping out with a lot of partying when the old people left. I wish you could have seen your Aunt Betsy and Cousin Sydney dancing on the tables!

Love, Mom

◆   ◆   ◆

Mom, we are so lucky to have been born into such a family. My aunts were all like mothers to me, and my cousins seemed more like brothers and sisters. It's a real comfort to know that your sisters are taking care of you, coming to Montreal when I died and, months later, giving you honest answers when you ask them honest questions.

I'm so glad I managed to leave Kamp Kanawana for a few days to come to the Torge family reunion last summer in Indiana. I almost didn't make it, as you know. It seemed like such a complicated trip for only four days. But luckily you told me it was a "command performance" and paid for my ticket, allowing me to be part of that warm, crazy group of relatives one last time.

Please remember that my cousins are having a hard time with my death, just as I did with Drew's. They may need you, as an aunt and a second mother, a little more than before.

Sam

THAT DAMN BACKPACK

September

Sam,

Your father and I have a little dance we do over the phone. Whenever we speak, he ends the conversation with: "When do you want to get together and go through Sam's backpack from Africa?" I always hesitate and then answer: "I'm not ready yet. Soon." Finally, knowing this can't go on forever, when he asked me again in September, I replied: "OK. I guess it has to be done. How about next week?" There was a long silence on the other end of the line and then ... "Actually, I don't think I'm ready yet. Soon."

In fact, we looked at everything in the backpack once. That was about a week after you died. Lenny and I went down to his basement and sobbed over every dirty sock, wrinkled shirt, and half-used toiletry item we found in there. I took an African necklace and gave it to Ariane, your girlfriend. We took out your wallet and papers in case we needed information from them. We each glanced through your diary once, but some of it was so personal that we didn't linger there. We read the sympathy cards, stuffed in at the last minute, from the day care teachers. But then we put it all back, and it's been living in Lenny's basement ever since.

I know it's not important to you anymore, but I care deeply about what happens to your stuff. At the same time, my caring doesn't seem to give me many hints about what to do with it all. I only know that I can't take it all over to the Mile End Mission.

Some items should be saved for your nieces and nephews when Riel, Patrick, and Rochelle have children: "Here's your Uncle Sam's wrestling sweatshirt and his purple satin Lakers jacket. He loved sports, have we told you that? Let's go look at his picture. You would have loved your Uncle Sam." Even though I picture this moment clearly, who am I kidding? It won't happen for another twenty years—those are things for a teenager, not a six-month-old baby. Will the Lakers still be around? And who ever heard of sharing a nostalgic moment with a teenager?

Your cousins have said that they would like a memento of you, but I will have to go through all your stuff to find the appropriate gift for each one. And looking at everything means feeling overcome by your presence. Besides, the odds are good that once I start in, I will want to keep it all close to me, not give things away.

Eventually Lenny and I will have to rummage through the backpack, and I will have to take down the containers in the pantry. Just as a spouse has to clear out the clothes from a dead partner's closet, I must decide which possessions of yours to keep and which ones to give away. But I'm so scared that I will make the wrong decisions.

When someone we know decides to plant trees one summer, I want to give that person your gear. I would feel sick if I threw it away. And all your little papers in that cigar box … they're all I have left of your handwriting. Do I save one of them or all of them? Besides, the junk in the box also reminds me of all the "nests" you made around the house. I still come across your seizure pills: one that has rested unnoticed under your bed for many months. I put it in the little basket with some of your pocket change, old key rings, and a ticket stub from a jazz concert. How long can I wait to clean out the drawer where all those loose ends now reside?

Riel has taken over your hooded sweatshirts, and I have, indeed, adopted several of your sweaters. There were no decisions made there; it just happened.

But I just can't see myself ever being in the right frame of mind to tackle the rest of your stuff, waking up one morning and saying, "OK, today I'm going to organize Sam's belongings." Even with my obsession for neatness, why would I ever want to do that?

Love, Mom

◆   ◆   ◆

Dear Mom,

Well, you're sure in a pickle on this one. I could give you the obvious plati-tudes—"It's only stuff and doesn't matter." "The real mementos are in your heart, not what's left behind."—but it all sounds a little lame when you're actually faced with a pile of clothes and a backpack from Africa.

I do think that there will come a time when deciding what to do with my stuff is not as painful as it is now. When you feel sure that memories of me will always be there for you, my socks and scribble notes will not be as important. I will be in your life as a spiritual companion who doesn't need to have warm feet or a piece of paper with a phone number. Then you might want to save one shirt that still has a faint smell of me or an old Valentine card I sent you. But these souvenirs should bring you happy memories, not sad thoughts.

Or maybe, when you're feeling stronger, you could put all my stuff in one place, like a dresser, and then take things from it when the time is right. Gather a pile of stuff for the cousins when you're driving down to Ohio for a visit. When my friends come over, invite them to take a peek and choose some-thing from my inventory. Keep your ears open for anyone going tree-planting or starting to wrestle—I believe my gloves, jersey, and helmet are still in the house.

As far as I know, there is no deadline for clearing out a dead person's belongings. Hold onto those things that bring you the biggest smiles. Let the rest of them slowly disappear into the lives of people I knew or strangers who need the stuff more than I do.

Sam

YOUR ASHES

September 19

Sweetheart,

We scattered your ashes today. It was the most miserable day of my life.

We gathered as your family: your Grandpa Herman and Carol were up from Ohio; Shirley came; Lenny, Marlene, Patrick, and Rochelle; Auntie Rozie and Laurie; Auntie Judy and Uncle Murray. And of course, Riel and I came. We had no plan about what we were going to do—that was the one thing we had decided: no organizing, nothing formal … just all of us together and your ashes in that box.

We drove up to Kamp Kanawana. It was a cloudy day with a warm breeze. Nature seemed to be lounging in bed with a book, waiting for us. Everything about the day was soft: the rustle of the leaves, the gentle swish of the lake, the diffused light from the clouds. Although I don't know Kamp Kanawana like you do, it seemed right that we were there. I felt very welcome in this place you loved so much.

You would have been one of the first to chuckle about the fact that your dad was late. Like you, I have never known him to be anything but early. I wondered, as we waited, whether he was reluctant to take you out of the closet and bring you to a resting place. He had joked several times over the last few months that he kinda liked having you there, among his shirts and pants. I knew what he meant.

We all stood around the fence that you and the kids had built last summer. Someone had planted young, upstart saplings on the other side, and it looked like a good place for you to be—helping the trees grow near the fence, next to the path where campers run back and forth from the dining room to their cabins. It wasn't in the middle of everything; it was off to one side, sort of like being with the kitchen crowd at a big, noisy party.

Your dad started off by reading a letter you wrote from camp when you were maybe seven years old. Do you remember it?

> Dear Patrick, Dad, marlene
>
> are you haveing fun, and I miss you too. I love you so much I have a story for you There was a boy called Sammy. he missed his family so much. so on viseting Day he saw his family. so he was so happy and live happy ever after. The End
>
> *And on the back of the letter:*
> I din't wet my Bed this time. Nobody calls me names.

Although you were really young, that letter captured the essence of you. We were all laughing and sobbing by the time Lenny finally got through it. I certainly hope you were aware of us then. The love we were all feeling for you was something I would want you to know and feel, no matter what form you are in now. It was pure and all-encompassing.

Then each person took a handful of your ashes and scattered them over the young trees. Some people spoke about you; others just held the ashes for a moment and then flung them over the plants. I told you how hard I was working to accept your death and how difficult it was because of how much I missed you. I promised you I would try harder still.

After months of learning how not to cry, we all gave in and let the tears flow: soft, wet drops on our cheeks, broken voices, pained expressions of grief and disbelief. The now-familiar feeling of surrealism covered us, and in our tears was the absolute surprise of your death ... once again.

After we had each done our scattering, there were still lots of ashes left in the box. These we took down to the dock, and again people took handfuls, this time letting them fall into the lake. The ashes mixed with the water in delicate patterns, sinking slowly, sinking wide. We commented to each other that it felt good for you to be part of the lake, but why we thought this I do not know.

When we had finished, it was clear that no one wanted to leave. We walked up to the picnic tables near the dock and told stories about you.

Lenny spoke about the time when you, maybe nine years old, were with the family in an Ottawa hotel when the fire alarm went off. Everyone was going out the door, but you couldn't find your shoes. After much searching, you found them, and as you were walking downstairs, Lenny explained how this experience demonstrated why it was important to keep track of things: if you needed something in a hurry, you could go straight to it. After a few minutes outside, you all went back to the room and to bed. Ten minutes later, the fire alarm rang again. As everyone scooted out the door, Lenny asked you, "Where are your shoes?" You proudly pulled back the covers to show him you knew just where they were: on your feet.

While we talked about you, I noticed that although our shoes and pants had ash spatters all over them, none of us wiped them off. The ashes on our hands, we rubbed in. I liked the dusty feel of them on my palms and hoped that some would seep past my skin into my body.

It was like touching you one last time.

I love you.

Mom

◆   ◆   ◆

Mom,

Thanks for letting part of me stay at camp. It's not just a physical place that I love. It's also where I grew up, learned to be a good friend to kids, fell in love, and laughed so hard my stomach hurt. I know that people appreciated me throughout my life, but at camp they never let me forget it. As I was planning my trip to Africa, I went off to camp that last summer, a little scared about the journey. I came back from camp knowing it was the right thing to do. I got a lot of strength there. I learned to believe in myself.

Besides, I like to think I'm scattered over a place where kids never have to change their clothes if they don't want to.

Your Boss-man, Sam

Ramblings …

As the date for scattering the ashes approaches, I try to find a way to ask Lenny if I can keep some behind. If I ever go to Africa, I want to scatter ashes there to keep Sam's spirit strong.

But I'm worried that this desire might mess with my own sense of closure. Although Lenny thinks it's fine, I wonder if it isn't a bit gruesome, even illegal, to keep someone's ashes around the house for longer than a year or two.

The morning of the event, I steal to the kitchen and take a small plastic container out of the cupboard. I even look over my shoulder as I put it in my purse. I know that if I can't sneak the ashes without being seen, I will come back empty-handed.

At the beginning of the ritual, when Lenny suggested that I come forward and take the ashes that I wanted to keep, I was mortified. I could feel my face getting red as I blushed. I fumbled in my purse for the small container I had brought and then explained this irreverent behavior to the others: I wanted to take Sam with me if I ever made the journey to Africa. The others smiled as if I were doing something grand, not stealing part of Sam for a private, selfish reason.

Why was I so worried about this? Where did I get such bizarre ideas about what can and cannot be done with ashes? I don't remember ever thinking about it, but the guilt I felt when I slipped that container into my purse was very deep and very strong. I am grateful that Lenny did not feel the same way.

So he sits beside my bed. Every once in a while, I open the box, take some ashes, and rub them into my fingers.

THE NEED TO BELIEVE

October

Sammy,

After almost sixty years on this planet, for the first time I feel the need to believe something about life and death. Why I didn't consider this important issue when Mom died is curious to me. I missed her deeply; I mourned her loss to the family. After all, she held it together. What would become of us? I felt orphaned. Even though Dad was still there, he was neither our caretaker nor our confidante; he could not be an older sister to me, the eldest daughter. All I remember was feeling that Mom was "up there" somewhere, looking down. And that seemed to be enough.

With you, it's different. I need to know what happened to you. Where did my child go? How do you exist now? What are you doing? It's similar to my need to know what you went through when you were sick in Africa and on your deathbed. I want something to hold onto so I can visualize you right now. It doesn't really matter to me whether or not it's true. But I can't move on until I know you're OK.

I hold some half-formed ideas about life and death that I've been gathering for many years but I've never explored my thoughts to see if they make any sense. I know you can't help me with this—you've already made that clear. But I will share them with you, nonetheless. You are, after all, the reason I am approaching this murky territory.

I always thought reincarnation was a good possibility. Regardless of the spiritual world's infinity, I could never quite grasp the idea of a space holding the souls of all people who have died since the beginning of time. Recycling souls—sending them back to complete unfinished business—seems more active, more purposeful, a more economical use of the spirit world. I like the cyclical aspect of this idea and often wonder what purpose I have on this earth to move my own soul path forward. But when I think about you and reincarnation, I don't get very far. Perhaps I have too narrow a picture of you—you're my son, pure and simple. Who you might have been before or what you might have to complete in the future … these ideas are just blanks in my mind. Maybe I will warm up to a reincarnated you later on, but it doesn't fit at the moment.

The life cycle concept has a lot going for it. In this scenario, you have returned to being part of nature. Your spirit is in the wind, the sound of birds, the snow and cold that coat our city in the winter. I sense a lot of truth here and have even experienced an awareness of you in the country, where nature seems more than just biology and science. Again, however, there's something inconsistent if this idea is the whole picture. When a breeze blows or the lilac tree sends a strong, lovely scent onto the porch, it is only you I feel coming toward me. Not Delano or Aunt Allu or Mom or anyone else I have loved who has died. Where are they, and why is my feeling of spirit so specific to you? I can only assume that this is a door I am opening for you … but not an explanation of what happens to everyone.

A few months ago, I read *The Five People You Meet in Heaven* by Mitch Albom. This book offered the idea that when a person dies, his soul meets up with five people (souls?) whose lives he has strongly influenced for better or worse. It's a variation on the concept explored in the movie *Flatliners*, where a person's soul must confront those he or she has hurt or harmed before that person can die in peace. What I like about these notions is that they suggest that you have something to do, another journey to make after this one on earth. I don't even pretend to know what people or events you might be dealing with, nor do I feel that I need to know. And let's be honest: it says more about me than anything else that I find comfort in your being busy rather than just hanging around meeting other souls (although I would never deny you the opportunity to run into Jim Morrison, Jerry Garcia, or Rocket Richard).

There is another sphere of being to which I have been close while writing this book. Your letters to me come from a place I do not inhabit. While I'm constantly writing down notes and ideas to include in my letters to you, your letters write themselves and need very little editing. Your voice is obviously not the same Sam who lived, but it's clear and it's you, all the same. Sometimes when I have finished my own letter, there is silence, and I just move on to another chapter. Am I opening the same door that lets you come in with the smells of summer? Is this a connection between those of us still living and those who have just died? Is this one of your ways to stay with me until I can let you go? Do you do this with Riel and Lenny as well? I believe the answer is yes to all these questions.

Your death has also shaken up my beliefs about life and its purpose. Unlike with these new thoughts on spirituality, which I have ignored until now, I did regularly take a step back and evaluate my life. I would reflect on whether I was on track, moving forward or backward, and accumulating the right kinds of experiences. However, when you died, things got royally screwed up.

First, I had never included in my life plan anything as important as losing a child, partner, or close friend. Why didn't I ever measure the worth of my life by whether my children were happy, my friends and my sisters were close, and everyone was still alive and healthy? If I had looked at my life through a different lens, would your death have been so shocking? It would have still rocked me in a serious way, but maybe I would have understood that life and death are always linked and that one must be aware of both.

Second, I've had to reevaluate the role that my work plays in my life. For many years, especially after you and Riel had started your own independent life journeys, I judged my success and failure on the basis of my various career paths. Was my work exciting? Did it make a contribution, no matter how small, to society? Your death has shown me that life is a lot more than work. What about creative projects? And learning new things? And having fun with friends? And traveling the world? And helping others who are less fortunate than myself? When I look at all my choices about how I could spend my time, I suddenly see that I have fashioned a very narrow life.

I know it's crazy, but I want to thank you for forcing me to reflect on these issues. I still have more questions than answers—why, oh why can't I just take up an off-the-rack religion and be done with it? As I explore my beliefs, though, perhaps I can make some peace with your death and start building another life that I am proud of.

Your Mom

◆   ◆   ◆

Dear Mom,

You have never been very good at living with loose ends. If there was no clo-sure—to a failed relationship or an unrealized project—you would still create a conclusion you could live with. This is just part of your character, and you will do the same with my death. As I've said before: dying is life's greatest loose end, and all the religions in the world and all your answers are merely specula-tions about a place you can never know until you are there.

That being said, I can understand your need to construct a system in which most of your questions are answered and the path ahead is clear. But in my own mind, I think asking the questions and testing the path are more impor-tant than finding answers or declaring a purpose.

And in that effort, I am happy to have helped you.

Sam

NEWS YOU CAN'T USE

November

Samuel,

Every time something happens that would be important to you if you were here, I send a little mind-message so you can pick up on it. But sometimes I don't have much faith that you're watching all these ups and downs from your new home. Just in case you weren't listening at the time, I'm putting the news here. There's no question in my mind any longer that you're with me as I write.

Melanie was in New York a few weeks ago and saw the woman who played "Molls" on the *Ed* show. Knowing this was your favorite TV program, Mel just had to stop her. She told Molls she knew someone who was a very big fan. They spoke about you, how you died, and how we had had special instructions to tape the programs for you while you were away in Africa. Mel described to her how you laughed to the point of tears during some of the antics on the show. The show has been canceled, so I bet your appreciation made Molls feel good. I guess they couldn't continue without you in their audience.

There have been quite a few other deaths and tragedies to deal with since you died. Delano finally passed away from his cancer. He is still, in memory, the coolest person I have ever known, and Melanie and I really miss him. Aunt Allu gave up the ghost right before Easter and finally got out of that terrible rest home. I went to Ohio for her funeral and spoke at the service about her unsurpassable fried chicken and the hundreds of felt-tipped pens she always kept in the drawer by her La-Z-Boy chair. Charlie Carroll died suddenly a couple of weeks after his eightieth birthday. I know he was like another grandfather to you, and we are all missing his bad Rodney Dangerfield jokes. Pam's daughter Jenna was in a very bad car accident in Mexico. She was in a coma for a while, and although she is now conscious, she is having to relearn how to speak and walk.

There was a hockey strike this season, so there have been no Canadiens games. At first there was a lot of talk and debate about it. Now everyone is just fed up with the greed on both sides and has taken to watching junior A games when in need of a hockey fix. I often wonder what you would think and what position you would take … although, if I take a moment, I can actually hear your anger about not having the games to watch, regardless of who's right or wrong.

Your girlfriend, Ariane, decided to go back to Kamp Kanawana this year as a counselor. It was her way of getting back on the horse after being thrown. During one of the session breaks, she came to Montreal and stayed at my place. It was lovely to see her. I asked her how she was holding up, and she said she found it hard but tried to remember all the good things about you—she might be smarter than I am in this regard. She was wearing the African necklace I sent her from the things of yours that came back. She said she never takes it off. Sam, she is really a lovely girl, and I am so happy you two had some time together.

I guess that's it for now. Sorry if it's all old news to you.

Mom

◆　　　◆　　　◆

The news is old but your version of events is most welcome. I don't experience these things anymore but do feel very present at each occurrence.

I wondered briefly if there was any power here to help get this hockey mess sorted out, but none of the decision-makers seem to be listening to any sense, practical or spiritual. I can truly say I am glad not to be around for all the bickering. I loved hockey, and it would have been very depressing to go through a whole season without it.

Sam

CRYING—PART II

November

Sammy,

I thought at one point I would never stop crying. Now I wonder if I will ever start again. It's not that I'm completely dry-eyed, but my tears are few and far between.

Sometimes I get sobs which come in intense half-bursts. When I pass your picture in the hallway and realize you're never coming back, a flood quickly swallows my body and I begin to wail. Then, just as fast, a floodgate comes up and cuts off the torrent. And that's it; it's over. No Kleenex needed.

I know this is probably not a good sign. A therapist would say I'm repressing stuff that needs to come out. But when I remember how exhausted I was when the crying was in full bloom, I prefer this half-strangled state.

Then there are the silent tear cascades. I never experienced these during the first few months of mourning you, but now they come every time I go to a funeral. Especially at Paperman's, when they have that magnificent cantor whose singing fills the hall with the sounds of death. While others look sad, I have sheets of tears falling down my face. It seems that your death has opened a door to everyone who dies.

Sometimes I think I've traded crying for living in a trance. I remember when the only thing I could do to get away from painful thoughts of you was to watch TV. Untangling the plots and figuring out who did the crime on those stupid cop shows and legal dramas gave me a tiny respite from pain. It made sense at the time. But many months later, as I continue to go there every evening to fill the time between work and sleep, I'm sure there's a real tornado brewing that's going to blow me away some day.

I feel guilty that the crying has stopped and hope you don't take it as a sign of the end of my sorrow. Crying is no measure of what I feel.

Remember how I shut down around six every evening right after you died? Maybe this is the feature-length version of the same film.

Mom

◆   ◆   ◆

Mom,

First off, crying is really overrated as an expression of pain and sorrow. Yes, it's one of the things people do when they are sad. But it is only one of the things. They also get angry, sell their houses, change their jobs, give up, scream, laugh nervously all the time, and fall into silent depressions. From up here, it all looks like sadness, no matter what the behavior.

Don't you think I see your feelings when you are watching Law and Order or CSI? I know you've watched some episodes twice without being aware of it until the very end. You may think you're trancing out, but I see you resting from a mammoth blow that life has just dealt you. Yes, a tsunami is definitely brewing, but you will be ready to hold your own when it comes.

I find it touching how you cry at funerals. At those times you are very close and receptive to the spirits of death. Others in mourning might stay away from such events because it would open their wounds. But you go, wounds and all, to places where death is the centerpiece, and open your heart. The cascade of tears is a wonderful expression of sorrow for someone who has just gone. It has the grace of a beautiful fountain. It shows silent respect for the dead.

You're doing O.K., Mom.

Sam

NO GRIEF GROUP FOR ME

November

Sam,

I hope you'll understand, but I have a real aversion to going to a grief group. Part of me feels bad about this because I know I belong with other parents who have lost their children. We are definitely a group in the true sociological sense of the word. We share a life-shattering experience. We have pain that is indescribable to anyone who has not been there. This is a group that welcomes new members but is never happy to see them arrive.

But I can't imagine getting together with these people just to talk about "it," hearing story after sad story of young lives cut short, listening to tales of anguish and inner turmoil. In an atmosphere of heavy sorrow, I might dredge up memories I want to forget.

Then there's the problem of dealing with the way most other parents talk about their dead children. To hear the stories, you would think that most of these children lived and died as saints. All of them were "special," never normal, everyday kids. They all had infectious smiles, sparkles in their eyes, and generous and kind natures. I rarely get any sense of the child's real character. They all seem to have the same story with only slightly different details for the same ending.

The few times I have encountered another grieving parent, I found myself in a competition over our dead children. Your smile was more infectious, your courage more grand to go to Africa, how many people came to *your* service. Each time, I've walked away disgusted with myself. Why can't I just give them a real, unairbrushed picture of you?

For me, grieving is a loner sport. It's an internal experience that has as many versions as the number of people forced to go there. Comparisons seem useless as a form of support. When I imagine myself in one of these groups, I can't see how will it help me to hear that this person couldn't get out of bed for six months. Or that another took solace in his or her three remaining children and was feeling rather good now.

I'm not judging those who find comfort in grief groups or take consolation from the special qualities of their dead children. But I don't understand how either would give me relief from this pain.

Perhaps I'm being rebellious even in my mourning: the status quo be damned, I'll do it my way.

Mom

◆　　◆　　◆

Dear Che Guevara,

Yes, there's a little bit of the rebel in your dismissal of grief groups. But if you'll permit me, I think you're missing the point. When I see these meetings and look at all those parents who, like you, have lost a child, I see them comforting one another. Comfort from someone who knows the depth of their pain. Hearing about one unique journey does not necessarily teach another individual how to feel or act. But the stories are filled with acts of courage that can inspire others to keep going.

You're in hand-to-hand combat with yourself over the facts: I have died and you are a grieving mother. Perhaps when you've come through that battle, you will want to tell someone about it ... someone who's been there and done that and knows what you were feeling.

Sam

GOING TO A SHRINK

December

Dear Sam,

I don't know what you'll think, but I've decided to go into therapy for a while. Although it's been many months since you died, I still feel like I am walking through sludge just to get to the end of a day. I have very little energy for my work, and I have no idea what to do when my workday is finished. I think I might be in a depression, but maybe it's just how a person feels when they lose a son. I'm hoping a shrink can help me figure it all out.

Thankfully I have found a good one, and there's a lot of new stuff to consider. If nothing else, he is asking me questions that even my closest friends and family wouldn't dare to pose: Why do you think you can produce your grief as if it was a television program? Who's taking care of you through all of this? Besides sadness and grief, what other feelings do you have in the course of a day?

One thing I've learned is that even though your death knocked me off my feet, it is my life, not yours, that has to be put back together again. After years spent perfecting certain habits, routines, and survival tactics, I see that some of this behavior is standing in the way of my dealing with your death. Like always doing everything myself, without help from others. Considering a day unproductive if I don't complete everything on my list. Judging my life by how well I'm doing at work. These practices might have made sense in my other life, but now they just bring me down.

I've always considered myself a fairly sane human specimen, but your death makes me wonder if I've got the strength to get through this. I can see why people often make huge decisions after their child dies—divorce, career change, even suicide.

I'm sure you're happy to know you're not the total cause of my mental disarray. I've been sliding along for several years now, ignoring the mysteries and hard knocks that a well-lived life is full of. A little tinkering on my neuroses might just bring back the spring in my step.

Your crazy Mom

◆　　　◆　　　◆

You've always had the energy of three people, so maybe it's your expectations that make you feel so slow and sluggish. I bet that if you did a survey, you'd find that most people who lose children do not spring back to full throttle within the first year.

I might have pooh-poohed a shrink when I was alive, but if it helps you, why not? I know my death is a big monster to handle, and some outside coaching can be an asset in your corner.

Who IS taking care of you now?

Sam

PLANNING CHRISTMAS WITHOUT YOU

December

Sammy,

Well, the dreaded holiday season is upon us. In November, when I saw the early birds putting up their Christmas lights and the pine trees arriving in the park, I wondered exactly what the "dreaded" part might be. Would I be sad every time I saw a Christmas sale? Would I want to buy you presents or break down on shopping trips when I saw stuff that would be on your list?

What actually occurred is not what I expected.

Whether it's wrapping presents or having a conversation with Riel about who will come to Christmas dinner, the usual excitement of the holidays has receded into the background like elevator music I don't really hear. What's moved to front and center is a very un-Christmaslike, dark absence that mingles with the bells, decorations, and shopping sprees. A hollow feeling surrounds everything I do. It's easy to remember things like mailing the presents to the family in the States—it's just a job for my automatic pilot mode. But taking out the lights and decorations, deciding on a Christmas tree, or getting the stocking presents requires a holiday energy that I don't have. I wonder if it will always be like this or just this year?

The most surprising change is how simple my Christmas plans have become without you in the mix. As you know, our holidays have always been a chaotic and busy time. Whether or not you and Riel were in town, there were dozens of conversations about what to get the cousins, Grandpa, and each other. I was on both your backs to get your Wish Lists to me so I could start shopping. You and Riel discussed my presents, and I advised each of you about what to get the other. We were all busy and running behind, so extra calls were needed as reminders that time was running short, packages had to get into the mail, and weird requests had to be searched for.

This year there's no bustle at all. There were a few calls between Riel and me about what we each wanted and what to get his cousin Briana. But now that the family packages have been sent, there's little need to talk and only each other left to shop for. In fact, I finished shopping for Riel two weeks before Christmas. I'm glad, in a way, that the stocking presents have slipped to the back of my mind, because doing them just before the big day may create a little bit of last-minute flurry, something I miss so much this year.

I've been trying to figure out some way to bring you into our Christmas plans. At one point, I thought I would scrap the traditional turkey dinner and serve up one of your favorite meals instead: Shake 'N Bake chicken, mashed potatoes, and corn. But Riel convinced me that it would turn a holiday dinner into a mourning meal, so we dropped that idea. I've considered doing a new-recipe gourmet dinner, serving a buffet rather than a sit-down meal, and inviting only a few instead of the traditional many guests. Anything that would change it into something different rather than the usual dinner, taking place without you.

What I can't seem to fathom, and what breaks my heart whenever I think about it, is the idea of never again having you at Christmas. It's the "never again" part that I can't handle. If it were just this year's Christmas that you were missing, I could cope. But I'm not ready to give up years and years of your not being part of the holiday hoopla.

Perhaps I will put out your stocking anyway and set you a place at the table. Would that be too weird?

Your long-time Santa

◆   ◆   ◆

Mom,

I'm also sorry that I won't be with you and Riel this Christmas. It was always a magical time for me, especially on Christmas Eve when, no matter where we were living in Montreal, we would both sleep over at your house so we could wake up together and open our presents in our bathrobes and pajamas.

Even though I won't be there, you and Riel should try to hold onto the things that make our Christmases so wonderful: the lovely glow of tree lights in the dining room; the smell of the turkey in the oven all day; your insistence, and our reluctance, about watching A Christmas Story for the hundredth time; the usual pattern of too many presents for us and too few for you; the arrival of Shirley's gang, Melanie, and "the boys" for a perfect meal, all the guys sneaking off to the TV room to catch a bit of the hockey game before dinner; a party of too many people crammed around too small a table, with at least one person who has never experienced your holiday feast or award-winning gravy; a rousing board game after the table is cleared, with an outburst from Riel because he hates losing and rarely wins.

It took us years to create this Christmas tradition, and I would hate to see it disappear just because of me. It's the essence of our family, and it must survive for Riel's children and for all those who have already come to depend on it.

You know perfectly well that there won't be room at the table for an extra place for me, and I know you won't have enough chairs even for the living. But I will be there in spirit, although I might just pass on watching A Christmas Story this year, since I finally have a choice.

Merry Christmas, Sam

◆   ◆   ◆

Ramblings ...

I remember my surprise when Sammy was born and I found out that parenting two kids was much more work than double one child. Besides the juggle of different demands from each, the interaction between them added a whole new dynamic to our lives. And Lenny and I had no alone, quiet time: when both of us were around, each had one kid. There was always too much to do, and our load seemed to increase fourfold.

This bizarre mathematical equation seems to also work in reverse. Now that I have only one son to attend to, the activity has decreased by much more than half. Besides having one less kid to consider in my plans, I've lost the dynamic between the two of them and the complicated, ever-changing relationship that was the three of us. I'm back to a simple, one-on-one relationship with Riel.

Is that why this Christmas seems so quiet and hollow?

A BETTER MOTHER FOR RIEL

January

Sam the Man,

I was taking Riel's clothes out of the washer and putting them in the dryer when I wondered if you were watching and remembering the countless times I refused to do that for you. The longstanding rule in our house—Start your own laundry; finish your own laundry—has gone the way of antiquated laws. He drops off his laundry with promises of coming back to change the loads, and I step right in, push it through all the cycles, and fold it neatly into his laundry basket.

I feel a bit guilty about doing this, but it brings out the mother in me, and I am desperate to find ways I can improve my parenting. It's not that I thought I was a bad mother to you and Riel, but I did have my shortcomings.

I don't think I put you at the top of my list as often as I should have. It would take me weeks to make time to help you with a project, my own work always getting priority time. The truth is that I obsessed about work, putting in long hours at the computer, often at the expense of your needs or the pleasure of simply hanging out with you. I wish I had been better at pushing my own tasks aside and putting yours in first place. When Riel needs to talk or wants curtains or bookshelves, I don't put him off. I try to respond quickly, in your honor.

I don't think I was a very good listener to you and Riel. When you would talk to me about difficulties at work or wonder why friends didn't call, I looked for solutions. You guys always accused me of lecturing you, and now I see you were right. My practical, *let's-figure-it-out* approach to

116

your problems didn't really fit when you were just trying to understand something. As your mother, I wanted all your problems to dissolve, all your heartaches to disappear, and all your confusions to clear up ... ASAP. But what you wanted, and what Riel still asks for at times, is just a compassionate ear, someone who loves you to witness the rough and tumble of ideas trying to sort themselves out. This is not something I do easily. Riel will attest that, though I am better, we still argue when I try to force a plan of action onto his *I-don't-know's* and *I'm-not-sure's*.

I am thankfully not crippled by regrets about how I treated you. I do feel bad, however, every time I remember picking up the phone after you had come into my office for a serious conversation. Why couldn't I see the hurt in your eyes?

I hope it's fine with you that I am only now dealing with this stuff. It's too late for you to benefit, but I guess you might be pleased that Riel might inherit a better mother.

Tell me it's so.

Mom

◆   ◆   ◆

Mom,

I'm glad that you're fine-tuning your motherly side. But you're forgetting the other part of the equation—Riel and I weren't perfect children, either. We often pushed you beyond your limits. We expected caretaking when we could have done things for ourselves. We would agree to cook you a meal but then wanted you to come up with the menu and keep us company in the kitchen while we were preparing it. We made very little space for you in your own house.

I often claimed you treated Riel better than me (and he claimed the opposite), but I know you loved us both, and I am happy to pass on to Riel whatever improvements I had coming.

If, however, you take a sudden interest in sports, turning off <u>Law and Order</u> so you can watch <u>Inside the NHL</u> with Riel, I'll be a little miffed even out here in spirit land.

Sam

THE FIRST ANNIVERSARY

January

My dear, dear Sam,

Today is January 13, 2005, exactly one year since you died.

For a few weeks leading up to this date, I've been worrying about it. What does it mean, "one year later"? How will it feel? What should we plan? Now I understand why people go to the cemetery on the first anniversary or finally bury the ashes: it gives them something to do on a day that must be acknowledged and commemorated.

I tried to rally Riel and your dad to come up with a good annual ritual. Frankly, I threw it their way because I didn't have any ideas. But they thought I was trying to organize them and rebelled. We finally decided to have dinner together, setting the table with your favorite foods … a good ritual in the end, one that I hope will survive for years.

Strangely enough, I woke up this morning around quarter to four. Just a few minutes after the exact time you died in Kumasi. I didn't fully awake … just made the connection, felt a pain in my gut, and went back to sleep.

I spent the day doing errands in the car and puttering around the house with you next to me. I allowed myself to think about you constantly, with no censorship at all. Yes, I felt the first day of the news. I brought back the images of you sick in the hospital bed. I spoke to a few people—Leslie in New York, Mickey in California. I went to lunch with Victor at your hang-out, Zorba's, and hugged the wife with the blond hair. I had my usual stick-and-salad, not your favorite souvlaki pita.

I know the "time heals" cliché has no meaning for you. As lowly human, however, I am encouraged by the number of wounds that are no longer so raw. Thoughts of you dead do not cripple me. My life seems real again, if not in very good shape. I am no longer afraid of forgetting you … in fact, you are nearer to me now than you were in those first few months of mourning. I can look at your pictures without an automatic feeling of horror that you will never be here again. I think of what a handsome guy you were, how cute that smile was, and how wonderful it would be to get a hug from you. I miss you terribly.

Anyway, Riel, Lenny, Marlene, Patrick, Rochelle, and Shirley will be here soon, and I have to get your garlic bread ready. Marlene's bringing your favorite lasagna (the one you claim only she can make), and I've had a go at some banana bread.

I know how much you love it when your entire family gets together. You're lucky to have one that can gather and have a good time. We'll make sure of it tonight.

Mom

◆   ◆   ◆

Mom,

I can honestly say that what you did on the anniversary of my death is exactly what I would want. To have you think of me all day with love. To have all of you sitting around the table eating my favorite meal. Kibbitzing with each other about this and that, my extended/blended family all getting along, a rousing debate about some news incident thrown in for good measure … that is the kind of evening that I found so precious when I was alive.

I know you were worried that no one spoke directly about me during the evening, but I preferred this joyous gathering rather than a sad one. Thank you for giving me another glimpse of a favorite part of my life.

Sam

Ramblings ...

One year later, my struggles and pain now a familiar part of my life, I hold onto several strong images of Sam that greet me randomly each day. I think of them as my personal picture book of a beloved dead son.

Sam standing in the office doorway in his flannel PJ bottoms, a sweatshirt with the hood pulled over his head, hands in his pockets, asking me to make him a pot of morning coffee at noon.

My son coming up behind me after an argument, turning me around, and saying, "I'm sorry," then giving me one of his awkward bear hugs.

The Canadian flag tattoo on his shoulder, his skinny legs, his strong back.

Sam sitting across the desk from me, confessing his frustration that things are not going well. His hands clenched as he tries to make sense of his life and what to do next, his expression simultaneously depressed and determined.

Sammy reading the sports section every morning with his breakfast, in his favorite spot at the table. Sitting with the boys in our living room in front of a Habs hockey game, proud of himself as he offers up player stats the others didn't know.

The two of us, sitting opposite each other at the dining room table, playing cribbage. Although I would win the odd game, he was a far better player than I was. How he loved that fact, especially knowing that I wasn't letting him win. A whimsical look on his face as he tried not to gloat, incapable of hiding the sheer joy of each victory.

A whiny but loud "Mom" yelled from two rooms away. He would be lying on the couch watching some sports program while I was completely involved in some work panic. Often I would ignore the first and second calls (or sometimes, so caught up in what I was doing, I didn't even hear him). It was his favorite way to irritate me. Finally, I would bite: "What, Sam?"

"Can you fix me a sandwich?"

And my answer, which he knew so well, waiting to see how pissed I was by the tone of my reply: "Are you nuts? Go do it yourself!" Almost every day I hear in my head that singsong plea from the couch: "Moooooommmmm."

My handsome son, perfectly dressed and shaved, ready for a night out. One last look in the mirror before he puts on his coat and walks out the door, always yelling to me over his shoulder, "Lock up after me, and don't wait up!" Then chuckling to himself (I have never waited up for him) as he sprints down the stairs.

COUNTING THE MARKERS

March

Sammy,

You've brought so many anniversaries into my life. Every time I turn around, there seems to be date to remember.

From the thirteenth day of the month, the day you died, I count backwards, making a quick note of how far—or otherwise—I've traveled. On May 13 (three months), nothing seems normal yet. On July 13 (6 months), it seems so far away, but I can still call up the shock at will. October 14: oh, my God, I went through the entire day yesterday without remembering it was the anniversary. I even wrote it in my notebook at the top of my To Do list, and it stayed on the page unnoticed. "Is this good or bad?" I ask no one in particular the day after.

At the beginning, I also counted the twenty-fifth day of the month, the day of the service, and always sat down to watch the videotape we made of the memorial. But after two or three times, I found myself fast-forwarding through the cassette, and the day was just another day of missing you.

Christmases will always be lonelier without you; there's no need to count how many. There will be a vacant space with no trimmings in our holiday house whether it's been one year or twenty.

It's your birthday, though, that cripples me. I wait for it with complete apprehension. This year I was working in Washington, D.C., when your birthday came around. I went into a coffee shop, got a drink and a birthday muffin, and sat by the window with you. I had hoped for a little nostalgia mixed with sadness during my silent celebration. What I got was a sick feeling in my stomach, a loss of connection with you, an out-of-body sensation that my roots to this earth had disappeared. My focus was shot, and I couldn't concentrate for the rest of the day.

I wondered why your birthday would be so unsettling and came to a surprising conclusion: Unlike the anniversary of your death, which marks a cruel event in the past, your birthday marks an absence of future.

As our lives move forward, yours stays stubbornly at twenty-five years. I can see that over the next few years—twenty-seven, twenty-eight, twenty-nine—it won't be so bad. My images of you and the pictures in the albums will still seem current. But when I'm seventy, Riel will be forty-two, and you would have been having your fortieth birthday. How will I imagine you then?

Will I have to create some fantasy of an older you? Imagine calling you on the phone because you're living far away? Or waiting for you to come over to the house for an extended family gathering in your honor? Would you bring a wife? A wife and kids? I guess I will have to look at Riel to get an idea of what you might have been. What other way would there be? I have no other signposts to guide me.

I know the smart thing to do would be to stop counting. The years after your death are not a measure of you but of us, the living.

But I can't help but wonder what my vision of you will be when I'm firmly in the old-age camp.

Mom

◆   ◆   ◆

Mom,

It's the counting thing that's screwing you up. You're right, you can't count for me anymore. I have become timeless, and that doesn't fit with the world you're in.

But timeless doesn't mean static. Look at how different I am already from the kid who died in Africa. I change along with you now. When you're eighty, I will still be Sam. And your memories of me will change as you age ... some-

times more boy than man, sometimes baby, sometimes teenager. You will see me in your grandchildren, and I will grow up all over again.

But no clocks will be ticking.

Your son, Sam

WINTER WARMTH

March

Sweetheart,

In the middle of our annual deep freeze, we're having a few days of warm weather. It's not T-shirt and sandal weather, but you don't need gloves and a scarf to go down the stairs for a quart of milk.

The first day the temperature rose, I decided to take the day off work simply to enjoy it. (I really am trying to get away from wall-to-wall work.) I went to lunch with Mary and had a coffee with Phiz, Shirley came for a short visit, and I washed the car. After weeks of caked-on snow, salt, and dirt, nothing can beat the rush of driving away in a clean car, looking out sparkling, clear windows.

At one point, I sat on the stairs and just basked in the sun. I watched the cars roll up and down Park Avenue. I watched people strolling on both sides of the street with their jackets open. Everyone was smiling, and most had a little skip in their step. I felt glad to be alive.

I thought about you. I imagined the excitement in your voice brought about by this little spring oasis. I pictured you getting off the number 80 bus, ball cap backwards, your jacket thrown over your shoulder, raising your face to the sky to soak in the warmth.

I felt your now-cosmic energy through the sun on my shoulders. I sat there for a good half hour, and the sadness never came. I was just happy that you were my son and we had so many lovely years together.

Mom

◆   ◆   ◆

You did it, Mom. You broke through to the other side.

This is how I will be with you from now on. Little snatches of me appearing out of nowhere: in the sound of a washing machine, a key in the door, a warm spot on the couch, a re-run of <u>Ed</u>, a bit of sun in the middle of winter.

And I can rest easy now, knowing that thoughts of me bring a smile to your face instead of tears to your eyes.

You are my best and favorite Mom, and I love you madly.

Sam

ONE LAST SAD FAREWELL

March

Dearest Sam,

I thought the previous letter to you was the last one. The way I imagined it, acceptance of your life and your death would come when I could think of you and find only warm memories instead of those sad, empty feelings that have plagued me for months.

But the strangest thing happened.

Whenever I told someone of that moment on the steps in the sun, huge tears came tumbling down my cheeks. The more I tried to sound hopeful and positive, the harder I cried.

Then I realized there were other good-byes to be said.

While writing this book and grappling with my grief, I have felt close to you in a way I never did when you were alive. During this most difficult time of my life, you have been my mentor, comforting and following me through territory that was rocky, uncharted, and certainly painful. Although I never felt you hovering over me or saw you in my dreams as I had hoped, you generously allowed me to hear your voice and gave me words of wisdom when I needed to see things more clearly.

I know that as I step to this other side of mourning, I have to let your guiding spirit go. It's a painful good-bye, and I'm not sure I'm ready to be there on my own. But when times are tough, I will try to remember the courage you had when you set off for Africa. I will never forget this time we spent together learning how to be apart.

So our relationship changes again. You will be with me in my heart, remembered in mind-pictures, smells, and sounds, not as a teacher but as my son once more.

I love you so much.

Mom

978-0-595-42383-5
0-595-42383-3

Printed in the United States
79736LV00003B/154-321

9 780595 423835